C000141025

1914 - 1918 Woolsery and Bucks Remember

Edited by Jonathan Downes
Typeset by Jonathan Downes, Jessica Taylor
Cover and Internal Layout by Jon Downes for CFZ Communications
Using Microsoft Word 2000, Microsoft , Publisher 2000, Adobe Photoshop.

First edition published 2015 by CFZ Publications

CFZ PUBLISHING GROUP
Myrtle Cottage
Woolfardisworthy
Bideford
North Devon
EX39 5QR

   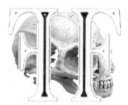

© CFZ MMXVI

All rights reserved. Without limiting the rights under copyright reserved above, no part of this publication
may be reproduced, stored in or introduced into a retrieval system, or transmitted, in any form of by any
means (electronic, mechanical, photocopying, recording or otherwise), without the prior written permission of both the copyright owners and the publishers of this book.

ISBN: 978-1-909488-47-2

Dedication:

To the people of Woolsery, past, present and future with love and respect

They went with songs to the battle, they were young,
Straight of limb, true of eye, steady and aglow.
They were staunch to the end against odds uncounted,
They fell with their faces to the foe.

They shall grow not old, as we that are left grow old:
Age shall not weary them, nor the years condemn.
At the going down of the sun and in the morning
We will remember them.

Robert Laurence Binyon (1869-1943)

THE EMPIRE NEEDS MEN!

THE
OVERSEAS
STATES

All answer the call.

Helped by the YOUNG LIONS
The OLD LION defies his Foes.

ENLIST NOW.

Woolsery Men who returned from WW1 August 1919

"And did you leave a wife or a sweetheart behind?
In some loyal heart is your memory enshrined
And though you died back in 1916
To that loyal heart you're forever nineteen
Or are you a stranger without even a name
Forever enshrined behind some old glass pane
In an old photograph torn, tattered, and stained
And faded to yellow in a brown leather frame"

Eric Bogle, *The Green Fields of France*

MEN WHO RETURNED FROM WW1 AUGUST 1919

#		#	
1		21	
2		22	
3	Jim Cook ?	23	
4		24	
5	**PERCY THOMAS**	25	....Perkins?
6		26	
7		27	Harry Prouse?
8		28	'CJ' Andrew?
9	**GEORGE MOORE**	29	
10	**WILLIAM CANN**	30	F. COURTENAY BURROUGH Of Woolfardisworthy Vicarage Your faithful Pastor and Friend
11	Albert Andrew?	31	
12	Albert Perkins?	32	
13		33	Jack Beckley? Albert Collings?
14		34	
15		35	**FRANK PROUSE**
16	**WILLIAM PENNINGTON**	36	
17	Albert Andrew?	37	Harry Prouse? Or James Walrond Burrough B.S.C Lieut. I.O.M.A.O.D ? see notes below
18		38	George Pickard?
19		39	
20		40	

Unfortunately people who do remember these men cannot recognise many of them from this photo. Number 37: It is also reported that this man could be **James Walrond Burrough** B.S.C Lieut. I.O.M A.O.D, Son of Rev. Courtney Burrough, if this was the case could Harry **Prouse** be number 27? But if number 37 is Harry Prouse could Lieut James Burrough be seated on his father's right hand side number 29?

Foreword

'I have been very affected by all the commemorations of the First World War, also called The Great War. If you consider that this was the first time sophisticated mechanical weapons were used in warfare, no wonder the death toll was so great. Many civilians also died in the intense fighting in villages and towns, innocently caught up in the fighting.

My father's eldest brother died at the Somme, aged 16. He ran away to join the army and by the time the family found him, he was dead. My grandmother never talked about it and kept a picture of him above her piano, as tribute, in 'the best room' i.e. the parlour.

So when we all argue about the value of war, we mustn't be confused with the sacrifice made by those young men who marched off to do their duty by us. Remember them in your hearts please, as all their mothers would want you to, and think of how they were cut down in their prime.

The politics are immaterial. They died for us.'

BARBARA DICKSON, OBE

REMEMBRANCE DAY

NOVEMBER 11TH

F.M. EARL HAIG'S APPEAL FOR EX-SERVICE MEN OF ALL RANKS.

Wear a Flanders Poppy

"If ye break faith with us who die we shall not sleep, though poppies grow in flanders fields."

BRITISH LEGION

APPEAL & PUBLICITY BRANCH

1 REGENT ST. LONDON. S.W.I.

Registered under the War Charities Act 1916.

Preface

"We will remember them"

In these Centenary Years of **World War One 1914-1918,** I wanted our community to mark this anniversary. Not to celebrate the War, but to remember the extreme sacrifice made by many families from our village. I decided that a *Woolsery WW1 Centenary Day* should take place. **Louise Leonard** came forward to help plan and organise the day, and with growing interest from the community we were able to create a deeper and more meaningful occasion than we had originally hoped for. **The Woolsery WW1 Centenary Day** was extremely well attended and raised great interest and passion within the local community and beyond.

The thought of a book became a possibility after conversations with a very enthusiastic and supportive local publisher **Jonathan Downes,** and **John Crossman,** former head of Woolsery Primary School; a keen local and family historian and researcher for the project. The three of us then put in many hours to draw the whole project together. I proceeded to collect artefacts and collate the information and photographs, pulling the whole project together. John researched the men, information about them and the environment in which they lived, and wrote the text of this book.

Jonathan then took over using his experience in the publishing industry to edit the book, assisted by Jessica Taylor. Jonathan produced the internal and cover layout, and this whole project finally came together in these pages.

Jane Cann
September 2016

Acknowledgements

There are many people who have supported this community project and our thanks go to them: *Terry Harding (local researcher), Dave Barbar (online researcher), Ian Arnold (local historian and medals expert), Brian Barrow (local historian), Matt Cole (current Woolsery School Headteacher), Cllr. Robin Julian (Devon County Council) who supplied a grant for the project, Janet & Chris Braund (The Braund Society who shared photos and family information), Gordon and Ted Lott (sharing their Uncle's war diary), Bideford and District Community Archive, Muriel & Richard Brine (Devon Heritage), Blundell's School Tiverton (Photo Credit for Mark Gilchrist Whyte).*

Finally we must thank the families of these men who have been prepared to share their moving stories, memories and photographs, and the community as a whole for their sincere support for The WW1 Centenary Day; the Church Service on the day was a very poignant public event, which is testament that *"We Will Remember Them."*

Introduction

Just how devastating The First World War was to the world, Britain and even our own community, has been brought to the fore by the centenary of the start of the conflict. 100 years is a long time to reflect and heal, but the tragedies and hurt have not been forgotten by many families. The suffering and huge loss of life is hard to comprehend, but the poppies displayed around the Tower of London between July and November 2014 visually captured the magnitude of the individual sacrifices for our futures.

I am sure we have *all* thought about the people in our families and communities who gave their lives, or those that survived the war. When reflecting, we find it difficult to fully appreciate what they went through. Those who returned home from WW1 were often wounded physically and mentally. It has been common to hear people say "they were *never* the same" when talking about a relative who fought in WW1. We know many of them did not - or perhaps more accurately, *could* not - speak of their experiences and memories, but we are grateful to those who did. It was while reflecting on these men and what they gave for our freedom, that Jane Cann and Louise Leonard of Woolsery began to develop the *Woolsery WW1 Centenary Day*.

What initially began as a small idea, quickly became far bigger; with interest and support from across the community, the success of this event was sealed. Many people helped with the organisation and research, while others came forward with items of incalculable sentimental value from their families.

Woolsery WW1 Centenary Day 20.09.14

When setting out to organise a community event such as *The Woolsery WW1 Centenary Day* it is difficult to anticipate numbers. We were humbled and moved when this community came together to remember. It has been both an honour, and at times very emotional to hear members of the community share with us their personal memories of family, friends, and acquaintances. People travelled from Bideford, Barnstaple and even as far as Salisbury and Glasgow to be part of the day.

The day began with three walks, passing through hamlets where these men had lived, and all met at the All Hallows Church in time for the service. Thank you to Chris Braund, Jan Ashworth and James Cann who led the walks. There were ten people walking from St Anne's, Bucks, more than twenty from Clifford and four started from Dipple, collecting more *en route* finishing at Woolsery with 27.

Special mention should go to Gordon & Ted Lott who both started from Dipple (the furthest point from Woolsery). Gordon's walking pace soon became too much for Ted to emulate, as he rocketed off to be the 'first finisher', but as Ted pointed out Gordon is younger! Both men, in case you didn't know, were in their eighties at the time.

The Church Service was very well supported with over 200 people attending. Thank you to Reverend Wendy Mitchell, and to Kevin Beer for putting together a very moving service, and to Mary Cann, Stuart and Val Snape & Derek Lott for all their time spent in preparation. We were delighted to have Armed Service personnel in uniform; Martin Momaghan the Hartland Royal British Legion flag-bearer, and Ben Brumham, the Hartland 326 Squadron ATC flag-bearer, as well as ten other ATC cadets all present at the church. The Woolsery Primary School children did a wonderful job of reading 'In Flanders Fields' and singing 'Make me a Channel of your Peace'.

Four of the ATC cadets who are descendents of some of the men in this book, read the roll call during the service. In the church stood the Woolsery WW1 Centenary Tree made by Ian Adams. On its branches hang replica ID tags which were painstakingly made by Martin Hill and his daughters Sharon and Donna (all from Woolsery) at Tazza Design in Bideford.

After the service there was a parade from the Church to the School, passing by houses in which some of the men who had fought in the conflict had lived. The parade was escorted by Mark Reed and his partner Bea, of the Royal British Legion Riders branch on a motor trike. We were privileged to have Lieutenant Colonel Robert Seymour of the Army Air Corps to lead our parade. Then came the flag-bearers, who were followed by local men and women who are serving, or who have served, in the Armed Forces, then ATC cadets and Brownies, and finally 111 people of our community who each carried a poppy to remember a man from the list.

Many thanks to John Richards (25035488 Sergeant Richards, late of The Royal Logistic Corps)

and Jack Johns (24726921 Staff Sergeant Johns, late of The Royal Logistic Corps) who organised the parade.

On arrival at the school Cyril Smith read a poem (see page 23) which he had written himself about his father in the war. This was a moving and fitting tribute for the day.

Instrumental to the day were the researchers who have spent hours and hours gathering and cross-referencing information about the men. Information and photos were on display for members of the community to view.

The Centenary Ceramics Project was a great success. 111 clay tiles were decorated and painted, each tile remembering one of the men. Thank you to Jax Williams from Tarka Pottery, Little Torrington who developed the ceramics project. The tiles were mounted as a mural onto the wall in the school hall; a wonderful reminder of a special day when Woolsery remembered - 100 years on - the men who left the village, some forever, to fight in what they believed was 'The War to end all Wars'. See appendix XX for a map of the tiles. The school was a perfect venue for the day's events, it being a hub of the village both now and 100 years ago, and also being where so many of 'our men' were educated.

Our local children were integral to the day, and thoroughly enjoyed the ceramics project. They were never bored with medal and poppy making, and playing on the Western Front Table with local childminder Sharon Bennett, and WW1 active storytelling and entertainment with Great Torrington School history teacher Bill O'Donnell.

We were delighted that, thanks to Cllr. Robin Julian, we were able to run the whole day for free, and leave two lasting legacies of the day:

• Community Ceramic Project

and

• This book with all the history

We have taken a lot of time and care in collecting and collating information and photographs, but we *know* there are more men whom we were unable to identify, and that the information we have may need corrections or additions, so if you have any further information or amendments please let us know.

Jane Cann & Louise Leonard

Come into the ranks
and fight for your King
and Country–Don't stay
in the crowd and stare

YOU ARE WANTED
AT · THE · FRONT

ENLIST TO·DAY

The Great War

The Politicians of the day were said to be the cause,
   As often throughout history, they've inflicted many wars,
   Fear spread between those nations near to the German border,
Then a chap called Ferdinand was shot, which brought chaos out of order.

Very soon with little warning, the battles did commence,
With soldier shooting soldier, which made things more intense,
In no time most of Europe was fighting foe to foe,
Then those who ruled Great Britain signed up to have a go.

"Your Country Needs You" was Lord Kitchener's famous cry,
But was it treating men like children saying "Come on, don't be shy"?
Then with just the basic training they went to the battle lines,
Where treacherous weapons awaited, such as shells, grenades and mines.

They also faced those massive tanks and live machine gun fire,
And trenches that were full of mud, just like a vast quagmire,
Yet those poor men that suffered had no means of redress,
For an unrelenting embargo was placed on the national press.

My Father was a soldier in the 14/18 war.
But he told us very little of the horrors that he saw,
With his right leg blown to pieces he lay upon the ground,
And mourned the loss of comrades whose bodies lay around.

That happened at Hill 60, somewhere on the Somme,
Where thousands upon thousands of men were too soon gone,
The suffering of survivors stayed with them deep inside,
And never ever went away, until the day they died

One wonders how these heroes got through their daily plight,
With all that devastation around them day and night,
Despite their awful hardships and the thought that they might die,
They'd sing the songs that were composed to keep their spirits high.

As you might guess, most of those tunes referred to their home life.
And how they missed their families amidst such needless strife,
One such song that meant a lot was based on a place called "Blighty",
Which for them felt, just like a prayer, said to Our God Almighty.

Blighty was another name for anywhere in Britain,
And occurred in conversation, or when letters home were written,
It was the dream of everyone to return again unscathed,
And pick up where they left off, but for this so few were saved.

It's now all a piece of history, from which lessons should be learned,
Yet 21 years later another world war returned,
And the tunes sung in the trenches were again on the lips of the brave,
But that's a theme for another poem, which for the future I must save.

Cyril Smith.

The WW1 Ceramic Mural at the School

The tiles are a beautiful reminder of a day the community came together to remember the 111 men who left our community and fought in WW1. The ceramic mural was unveiled by David (Jack) and Vanessa (Nessy) Johns in a school assembly on Armistice Day 2014

We hope the community will look at these tiles for years to come and remember the men who left their homes and all they knew to protect our freedom. It will also remind us that we came together as a community to remember them 100 years later.

Thomas Cruse & Harry Found	George Moore	Jas Wonnacott	John Prouse (Bodie Johns)	Charles Callaghan	James Bate (Jamie Blackwood)	Richard Stevens	Job Beer*	Harry Eastman	Richard Thomas & Mark Westaway
Bert Cole	Mark Braund*	JT Cruse	John Glover	Willam Bickle	Fredrick Wade	Samuel Colwill	Arthur Beer (Arthur Cann)	Stanley Jenkins	Percey Pengilly
Fred Eastman	JW Burrough (Matt Cole)	George Boughton	William Tuke	Victor Moore	George Cook	Seth Davey	James Bond	John Short	Samuel Searle
Harry Sanders (Harrison Rhodes)	John Peard	William Perkins	John Perkins	John Johns ('Jack' david Johns)	Ernest Dunn*	Thomas Pengilly	Harry Davey	John Manners	Harry Jewell
WJM Bennett	James Perkins	Albert Perkins	Mark Whyte	Edwin Stacey	Wilfred Andrew	William Braund	Richard Elwes	Dennis Braund	William Babb
Walter Dayman	Edward Peard	Llewellyn Pengilly	Walter Johns	Stanley Headon	CE Williams	Ernest Dunn*	EC Cornish	Leonard Sanders	William Beer
James Cook (Margaret Buckley)	Albert Drury	William Glover	Fredrick Johns ('Nessy' Vanessa Johns)	Richard Moore	Chas Gliddon	Charlie Peard	Charlie Davey	John Dark	Joseph Tyrrell
Edward Braund	George Pickard	Thomas Rowe	Job Beer	Alfred Thorne (Sophie Stevens)	Albert E Tranthen (Brian Barrow)	Cyril Andrew 'CJ'	Jack Beckley	W Hockin	Percy Hatch
Ernest Cole	Samuel Thomas	William Cudmore	Leonard Johns	Frank Tardival	James Somerville	Fredrick Jenkins	Archibald Stevens	Fred Shaddick	William Prouse
Lionel Prance	Joseph Braund	Frank Stanley Burrough	Albert Collings	Mark Braund*	William Stevens (Archie Stevens)	Joseph Carter	Ernest Glover	Fredrick Braund	James Thorne
Harry Prouse	George Brent	WT Howard	Thomas Headon	Wilfred Davey	James Shackson	Thomas Johns	William Pennington	Job Beer*	William Cann (James Cann)
Frank Corey Prouse				*Woolsery WW1 Centenary (1914-2014)* Remembering the men of Woolsery, Bucks and Clovelly who went to War					Albert Andrew

* indicates a man who has two tiles for his name

It is particularly poignant that the tiles are displayed on the wall of what was the only schoolroom when the men in this book went to school there. The tiles will remain on the wall of the school hall in perpetuity, as a memorial to the men and boys of our villages who went to war for us. Visitors are welcome by arrangement.

NB: Names in brackets are the people who created the individual tile.

Cadet Roll Call

Four of the Hartland 326 Squadron ATC cadets were descendents of three of the men we were remembering and it was a fitting tribute that they performed the roll call of the 111 men during the church service. Sophie Johns is a great great Granddaughter of Joseph Braund, Freya Hancock and Georgina Allin are great great nieces of Frank Prouse, Cory Harding is a great grandson to Harry Prouse, and his great uncles were Frank, Thomas & William Prouse.

Who have we researched?

We began our planning by looking at the Woolsery War Memorial in All Hallows Church, which is unusual as it lists 53 men, of whom only five are listed as having died. We have since found 27 more men who left to go to war, one of whom was Leonard Johns who was killed on the Somme, and is not listed on the Woolsery Memorial. As our search for these Woolsery men progressed we realised that there are few clear boundaries between Woolsery, Bucks Mills and Clovelly, and even Hartland as well. However, we had to draw a line in the sand from which to focus our research. We have kept our centre of attention on Woolsery, researching the men who died and those who returned. We have also included information on the men from Bucks Mills and Clovelly who died. The Spring 1919 Absent Voters List, kindly provided to us by Ian Arnold of Bideford, gave us additional names of men who returned from the war from Woolsery, Bucks Mills and Bucks Cross. For the Bucks Mills Memorial in St Anne's Church we have used information that was compiled by Jill and Chris Braund of the Braund Society, which is on display in the church. We have also completed some further research on these men. Information about the Clovelly Memorial was obtained from the Devon Heritage website, and WW1 local historian Brain Barrows gave us information on a further nine men who were from (or had links with) Clovelly, but are not on the Clovelly Memorial. John Crossman and Dave Barbar have researched ancestry and military websites, and Terry Harding has searched the local graveyards. Jane Cann, Louise Leonard and Terry Harding collected information from local people who are descendants of these men or remember them.

Our list includes a total of 113 men, of which 37 lost their lives to the Great War. That is five on the Woolsery Memorial, seven on the Bucks Memorial and sixteen more on the Clovelly Memorial, plus eight more Clovelly men who are not listed on the memorial and one man from Woolsery who died, but is not on the Woolsery Memorial. Job Beer is mentioned on both the Woolsery and the Clovelly Memorials, Thomas Johns is mentioned on the Woolsery and Hartland Memorials and Thomas Curtis Rowe is mentioned on both the Woolsery and the Bideford Memorials. We understand that not every family wished (or could afford) for their loved one to be remembered on a memorial, which means that we can never be certain to have all the men listed. Also, it is quite common for a man to be remembered on more than one memorial across the country depending on where he lived and worked, and where his family lived.

It should be pointed out that although we have spent hours carefully researching and collecting this information it does not mean it is all correct. If a man died there is usually a lot of information on him, but for those that survived it is more difficult to find historical records. Research is also made difficult by names that are used interchangeably like 'Harry' and 'Henry', or 'Jack' and 'John', and families that have father and son who go by the same name. We were unable to find *any* information on some men, and some records were poor or illegible. However, we hope that you find the information in this book interesting and thought provoking.

For the purposes of this book we have looked at the men from Woolsery, Bucks Mills and Bucks Cross, but have included the information on the Clovelly men in the appendix.

These men are listed on the memorial in All Hallows Church, Woolsery, those in bold died at war.

	Albert Andrew	Cranford
317158 PNR	Cyril Andrew 'CJ'	Fairholme Woolsery & Post Office
	Wilfred Andrew	Dipple Farm, Common Moor
216165 GNR	John 'Jack' Beckley	Pick Park, Alminstone Cottages, Stroxworthy, Melbury, worked Alminstone Farm & Walland Carey Est
	Arthur Beer	Church Park Cottage Woolsery worked at West Town Farm & Kennerland Farm
B/201888 PTE	**Job Beer**	Lived Church Park Cottage Woolsery, worked **Dyke Green Clovelly**
25046 PTE	**William Beer**	**Thornery Clovelly then Back Street Woolsery**
	WJM Bennett	
	George Brent	Village
	Frank Stanley Burrough	Vicarage at Cranford
	JW Burrough	Vicarage at Cranford
66351 PTE	William Cann	South Stroxworthy
	Jas Cook 'Jim'	Ford Cottage Alwington, the Sloo Parkham, worked at Howley Park Parkham and later lived in Forestry Cottages at Powlers Peice.
	EC Cornish	
	Seth Davey	Lane Mill
	Ernest Dunn	Ashcroft & Kesmeldon
	Fred Eastman	Marshall Gate
	'Harry' Henry Eastman	Marshall Gate
189103 PTE	Harry Found	Venn Cottage
	'Chas' Charles Gliddon	Stroxworthy
	Ernest Glover	Huddisford, Venn Lane
	John Glover	Bitworthy Farm
70019PTE	Percy Hatch	Village
	W Hockin	
	Stanley Jenkin	Working at Hotel Woolsery (Farmers Arms)
345911 PTE	**Thomas Johns**	**Seckington & Gorrell**
	Victor Moore	Cranford Water Cottage

238661GNR	George Moore	Stroxworthy then West Moor
Wheeler A. 145941	Richard Moore	Cross Park & boarder at Hotel (Farmers Arms)
A.B. R4620	John (Jack?) Peard	Village & Horns Cross
21700 PTE	William J Pennington	Lived Fairy Cross, worked Walland Carey Est
	James Perkins	Venn Farm, Green Cottage
	John Perkins	Venn Farm, Lane Barton, Canada
238662 GNR	William Perkins 'Bill'/'Willie'	Venn then in Village
640451 PTE	Albert Perkins	Venn then in the Village
	George Pickard	
	Lionel Prance	Alminstone Cottage
2326 PTE	Frank Corey Prouse	Built and lived at The Laurels
23369 PNR	Harry Prouse 'Plummy'	Lived Village & South Stroxworthy, worked at quarry opposite Strouds and milked cows at Irene
T2/016200 SGT	John 'Thomas' Prouse	Village
	William Prouse	Village
800 PTE	**Thomas Curtis Rowe**	**Elmscott Hartland**
	Samuel Searle	
	Fred Shaddick	Claw Cross, East Park
	Edwin Stacey	
T/422768 DVR	Richard Stevens	Huddisford Moor, Cranford, Sessacott
202285 PTE	**Archibald Stevens**	**Lived Huddisford Moor, worked Gorvin**
116979 GNR	Richard 'Percy' Thomas	Village, Cross Park
520223 PTE	Albert E Tranthen	Moorhead & Village
	Joseph Tyrrell	Back Street
98255 A/M2	Fredrick Thomas Wade	Ashmansworthy
	Mark Westaway	West Villa
	Jas (James) Wonnacott 'Jim'	Stoop Dyke Clovelly, Chapel Street

The following men are not listed on the memorial in the church but are on the spring 1919 Absent Voters List under the parish of Woolsery, or have been mentioned by local people.

2616 PTE	William Lewis Boundy	Cranford House, Woolsery
39000 PTE	Fredrick Braund	8 Bucks Mills
	Joseph Braund	Bucks Cliff
	William G Braund	Bucks Cliff Hotel
7676 PTE	Joseph Carter	Church Park Farm Bucks
66352 DVR	Bert Cole	Church Park Farm Bucks
	Ernest Cole	Walland Cottage Bucks
	Albert Collings	Fouchole, Woolsery
	Smal. Thos.	Sleep Cowling (Samuel Thomas) Venn Farm
246622 PTE	William Cudmore	Bucks Cross

202486 PTE	John Wesley Dark	Bucks Cross Post Office
39019 PTE	Harry Davey	West Bucks Whitehouse Farm
462717 PTE	Wilfred Thomas Davey	Sea Breeze Bucks & Church Park Woolsery
K14472 STO	Thomas Richard Headon	Hartland
	`Fredrick H Jenkins	Bucks Mills
267186 PTE	John Johns	Walland Cottage
248976 DVR	Edward Peard	Alwington & Goldworthy Parkham
227998 PTE	John Short	East View Cottage, Pleadymead & Myrtle Cottage
K31477 STO	James Thorne	Bucks Mills
332873 C.F.A.	Alfie Thorne	South Stroxworthy, Canada, 2 Cross Cottage Alminstone then was at Pick Park (Oakapple Cottage) South Stroxworthy and Cranford.
905 PTE	Fredrick Johns	Bucks Cross
280137 PTE	Walter John Johns	Burford, South Down Cottage Bucks
44680 PTE	Edward John Pickard	Bucks Cross
	William Glover	Venn
K31472	Mark Braund	7 Bucks Mills
15073/203721	PTE Charlie Peard	Braunton
20765 & 13480	Leonard Johns	Clifford Cottage, worked West Town
R27 799 CPL	Charlie Davey	

St Anne's Bucks Mills Memorial

9667 CPL	Dennis Braund	7 Bucks Mills
K/33252STO	Edward Braund	Bucks Mills
PTE 203572	Walter Thomas Dayman	Bucks Mills
	Richard Cary Elwes	Walland Cary
138312 Cadet	Harry Sanders	15 Bucks Mills
20371 PTE	Leonard Sanders	15 Bucks Mills
	Mark Gilchrist Whyte	Whyte Cottage Bucks

Clovelly Memorial C1-C17 and C18-C25 other men with links to Clovelly

20764PTE	William P Babb	Clovelly
B/201888 PTE	J.Beer	* As above on Woolsery Memorial*
53474PTE	James Bond	Hartland
45400SGT	Charles Callaghan	Huddersfield
15721PTE	S.amuel PColwill	Stoke
20815PTE	George Cook	Clovelly
AB	James T Cruse	Clovelly
AB	Thomas W Cruse	Clovelly
12/1416 PTE	Stanley B Headon	Bucks Mills
11478CPL	W.T.Howard	
102725 PTE	Harry Jewell	
37600	Llewellyn R Pengilly	HM Coastguard Station Clovelly
AB	Thomas S Pengilly	Clovelly
19867DVR	James H Somerville	Clovelly
4516 L CPL	William Stevens	Clovelly, Burscott, Mouth Mill, Ford's Farm Bradworthy

279894   Frank Tardivel
6384 SGT   William A.B. Tuke
                James Bate
                William Bickle
                George Boughton
                Percy William Pengilly
                James Henry Shackson
                C.E. Williams
                Albert Drury
                LT John Mann

The Great War 1914-1918

It is not easy to record the turbulent proceedings of one of the most tumultuous events in world history in just a few paragraphs, but it is necessary to try to outline the background, in order to give the reader some idea of the situation in which our brave heroes set out to play their part, and in some cases gave their lives.

On 28 June 1914, Archduke Franz Ferdinand of Austria, heir presumptive to the Austro-Hungarian throne, and his wife, Sophie, Duchess of Hohenberg, were shot dead in Sarajevo by Gavrilo Princip, one of a group of six assassins (five Serbs and one Bosnian) coordinated by Danilo Ilić, a Bosnian Serb and a member of the Black Hand Secret Society. The political objective of the assassination was to break off Austria-Hungary's South-Slav provinces so they could be combined into Yugoslavia. The assassins' motives were consistent with the movement that later became known as Young Bosnia. The murder led directly to the First World War when Austria-Hungary subsequently issued an ultimatum against Serbia, which was partially rejected. Austria-Hungary then declared war.

World War 1 began on July 28, 1914. The two opponents were the Entente countries, which included France, Great Britain and Russia against three empires, Germany, Austria-Hungary and the Turkish Ottoman. In total, 30 countries were eventually involved in the conflict. Italy, once part of a Triple Alliance with Germany and Austria-Hungary, fought on the side of the Allies. It ended on November 11, 1918.

This was a war that many - including the eminent war historian John Keegan, writing in his book *The First World War* - believe was unnecessary because the chain of events that led to its outbreak might have been broken at any point during the five weeks of crisis that preceded the first clash of arms. The fear at home was that if not fought it would allow Germany to rule Europe, an objective which was to be resurrected some two decades later, and which still worries some antagonists of the European Economic Community today.

The war ended after four years with a bitter legacy of rancour, not to mention racial hatred, all ending in another more terrible war twenty one years later, which killed five times as many people and caused a great deal more damage in material terms. Adolf Hitler roused his people by ranting "It cannot be that two million Germans should have fallen in vain. No, we do not pardon we demand vengeance."

At the beginning of 1914 the British Army had a reported strength of 710,000 men including reserves, of which around 80,000 were regular troops ready for war. By the end of World War I almost 1 in 4 of the total male population of the United Kingdom of Great Britain and Ireland had joined up, over five million men. Of these men, 2.67 million joined as volunteers and 2.77 million as conscripts.

For a century, British governmental policy and public opinion had been against conscription for foreign wars. At the start of World War I, the Army consisted of ten divisions and one cavalry division. 14 Territorial Army divisions also existed, and 300,000 were in the Reserve Army.

Lord Kitchener, the Secretary of State for War, considered the Territorial Army untrained and useless. He believed that the regular army must not be wasted in immediate battle, but instead used to help train a new army with 70 divisions, which was the size of the current French and German armies. This number, he believed, would be needed to fight a war lasting many years, unlike those who thought it would all be over by Christmas!

By the end of September, over 750,000 men had enlisted; by January 1915, a million. The reasons for their enlistment cannot be pinned down to a single factor; enthusiasm and a war spirit certainly drove some, while for others unemployment prompted enlistment. Some employers forced men to join up, whilst many certainly volunteered knowing that the war front would be a dangerous place to be, and many joined simply because it seemed to be a threat to their home and country. A majority believed that it would be a short and victorious campaign. Some industrial workers were encouraged by the offer of a pay supplement from their employers whilst they were away, although this would rarely have happened in the agricultural world.

Nationally, in 2014, great interest was aroused by the wonderful poppy display at the Tower of London, one poppy representing each commonwealth soldier who gave his life. 11.5% of British soldiers lost their lives to the conflict, not including those who died in subsequent years due to their suffering. Surprisingly 17% of officers were killed, thus perhaps disproving the belief that the working classes were the cannon fodder. Eton alone lost over 1,000 former students. Britain lost 2% of its total population to the war compared to just under one per cent in the second world wide conflict and 4% in the English Civil War of the seventeenth century. Serving soldiers actually spent about ten days a month in the trenches, and received 4,000 calories a day, being provided with meat every day as well as tea and rum, a rare treat for many a poor boy of the time.

They were also provided with cigarettes.

Sir Arthur Conan Doyle, creator of Sherlock Holmes wrote the following in an attempt to enrol sporting stars:

> "There was a time for all things in the world. There was a time for games, there was a time for business, there was a time for domestic life. There was a time for everything, but there is only time for one thing now, and that thing is war. If the cricketer had a straight eye let him look along the barrel of a rifle. If a footballer had strength of limb let them serve and march in the field of battle."

Many famous sportsmen went to war; 34 first class cricketers died as well as 26 England international rugby players including Ronald Palmer, the nation's captain at the outbreak of war. Countless names familiar to football fans also lost their lives. Lord Asquith, the Prime Minister, lost a son, Bonar Law, a future P.M., lost two sons, and Anthony Eden lost two brothers and a third was badly injured.

Famous writers who served included J.R. Tolkien, A. A. Milne and two who spent part of their lives in North Devon, Saki and Henry Williamson. Rudyard Kipling's only son, John, was killed in 1915 aged just eighteen. Adolf Hitler - a soldier who received the iron cross for bravery, and Herman Goering - a successful war pilot - were amongst the troops on the other side.

On the first major day of the Battle of the Somme July 1916 when Entente troops left their trenches to attack the enemy, Britain suffered almost sixty thousand casualties. To put that number into perspective that is about twice the number of people who compete annually in the London Marathon.

One early enrolment peculiarity was the formation of 'pals battalions': groups of men from the same factory, football team, bank, village or similar, joining and fighting together. The idea was first suggested at a public meeting by Lord Derby. Within three days, he oversaw enough volunteers sufficient for three battalions, in all probability about 1,500 young men. Lord Kitchener gave official approval for the measure almost instantly and the response was impressive. The drawback of pals' battalions was that a whole town could lose its military-aged men folk in a single day. These seemed to be more the precept of larger conurbations and so the local men did not fall into this category, but many joined the Royal North Devon Hussars as well as the County's own battalions! Over forty of the players and staff from Clapton Orient Football Club (now Leyton Orient) signed up for a pals battalion and marched off to war after defeating Leicester 2-0. Three of their members lost their lives on the Somme.

Perhaps not surprisingly, at the end of 1915 sufficient numbers were still not signing up and the French Army was in dire need of relief. This lead to a Military Service Bill being introduced in January 1916, providing for the conscription of single men aged 18–41; in May conscription was extended to married men. Over the whole period of the war, conscripts made up a majority of British serving soldiers. The government pledged not to send teenagers to serve in the front line. Ireland, which was still part of the United Kingdom at the time, was excluded from the scheme. Later proposals to introduce conscription in Ireland led to widespread support for Sinn Féin and independence. Conscription, however, had little impact on enlistment. The number continued to decline towards 40,000 a month, as essential men were needed at home for war work, and the poor health of many others remained a barrier, even as the requirements were progressively reduced. From 1.28 million enlisting in 1915, this had fallen to 1.19 million for 1916. In 1917–18 only 36% of men examined were suitable for full military duties, 40% were either totally unfit or were classified as unable to undergo physical exertion. In 1918, the British Army was actually smaller than in 1917 (3.84 million to 3.9 million) and almost half the infantry was nineteen or younger.

The categories of health levels for conscription or enlistment were as follows:

A : General Service.
B1: Garrison Service Abroad.
B2: Labour Service Abroad.
B3: Sedentary Work Abroad.
C1: Garrison Service at Home Camps.
C2: Labour Service at Home Camps.
C3: Sedentary Service at Home Camps.

The Official History records the physical standards defining each category:

A: Able to march, see to shoot, hear well and stand active service conditions.
B: Free from serious organic diseases, able to stand service on the lines of communication in France, or in garrisons in the tropics.
B1:Able to march five miles, and see to shoot with glasses and hear well.
B2:Able to walk five miles to and from work, see and hear sufficiently for ordinary purposes.
B3:Only suitable for sedentary work.
C: Free from serious organic disease, able to stand service conditions in garrison at home.

The war in Europe rolled on with inevitability until the final year when first the German allies made an all out attempt to break through and defeat their enemies on the Western Front, pouring in extra troops to break the line in what is now sometimes referred to as the Kaiser's Battle, although by this time Germany was being ruled more by its generals and less by their monarch. The timing was prompted by two major events. Firstly the war with Russia, who were more interested in consolidating their revolution, had ended freeing up many of the German troops to head west, and the impending entry of the United States into the war meant they needed a decisive thrust before it was too late.

Once this had been thwarted and the blockade on German ports was literally starving its population, the tide was beginning to turn. The humble turnip had become the basic food for many in Germany and the lack of rubber imports meant many of their battle vehicles were running tireless, whilst the lack of raw materials for weapons was also hampering their efforts. The allies had finally gained air superiority, and with the imminent arrival of American troops events were very much in Britain and its allies favour.

The great Australian general John Monash, a former civil engineer, who had seen success under his command in Gallipoli, now led the Australian forces, and it was his concept of warfare being conducted by foot soldiers supported by tanks and air power which proved decisive. His reputation as one who planned everything to the most infinite detail was long remembered; some recalled how he even managed to arrange for hot meals to be delivered to his troops in the heat of battle.

Whilst much is written about the trench warfare, and rather less about the battles at sea, the travails of our troops in the Middle East has had very little coverage. C.J Andrew was one who saw action in Palestine and returned, but Thomas Johns gave his life in the final days of the battle for Jerusalem in December 1917.

Back in Europe, the final Allied push towards the German border began in October 1918. As the British, French and American armies advanced, the alliance between the Central Powers began to collapse. Turkey signed an armistice at the end of October, Austria-Hungary followed on November 3. Germany began to crumble from within. Faced with the prospect of returning to sea, the sailors of the High Seas Fleet stationed at Kiel mutinied on October 29. Within a few days, the entire city was in their control, and the revolution spread throughout the country.

On November 9 the Kaiser abdicated, slipping across the border into the Netherlands and exile. A German Republic was declared and peace feelers extended to the Allies. At five o'clock on the morning of November 11 an armistice was declared in a railway carriage parked in a French forest near the front lines. The terms of the agreement called for the cessation of fighting along the entire Western Front to begin at precisely 11 o'clock that morning. After over four years of bloody conflict, the Great War was at an end. This meant that our heroes who had survived this conflict could soon return home to their families, whilst other families continued to grieve for their loved ones who had perished. Some returned home never to enjoy the levels of good health they had enjoyed pre-war and indeed suffered early death as a result of shell shock, the effects of gas warfare, and wounds. Some appeared to recover from their ordeal and lived long lives, but just how mentally scarred they were we shall never know. Some soldiers who had survived the conflict died of a particularly virulent Spanish flu which spread rapidly across Europe at that time, before they could arrive home.

Devon Regiment Battalions of the New Armies

It is clear that the vast majority of the village's heroes went into the army with just a handful joining the other services. Most of the soldiers were probably in the various Devon Regiments.

The Regiment on a route march in 1914

The following were among the battalions containing the new soldiers volunteering or conscripted into the County force.

- **The 1ˢᵗ Battalion Devonshire Regiment**.

A regular battalion stationed on Jersey when war was declared. They embarked on SS Reindeer and sailed to France to join the Third division soon in action on the Aisne at Vailly Sur Aisne by the end of the following month they had already suffered almost one hundred casualties.

They were transferred to the 14ᵗʰ Brigade of the 5ᵗʰ Division before moving to Flanders in October prior to the battle of La Bassee. An operation in the Givenchy and Festevny area suffered 60 casualties, with another 40 by the end of the month. They then joined the lines opposite Messines for the oncoming winter. Their next move was to Hill 60 at Ypres Salient; at around this time Dennis Braund was severely wounded. They continued in the trenches throughout that summer before heading for the Somme in July 1915, where they remained until spring 1916, prior to going to Arras, until - in July - they travelled back to the familiar environment of the Somme, now as part of the 5ᵗʰ Division. It is believed that they were just one of 616 Divisions fighting there. They remained there until November of that year and were involved in the attack on Leuze Wood and Morval before wintering in the Givenchy area. In the Battle of Arras they attacked La Coulotte and on 23ʳᵈ April lost over seventy men with over 160 wounded. This total casualty list of over 240 left them sadly depleted, but in the next weeks they were involved in the attack on Fresnay. They then moved to Arras in September 1917 before being transferred back into Belgium in the "Third

Ypres." The battalion was in action in or near Polygon Wood on 4th October and then the following month set off for Italy and wintered there before returning to France in March 1918. In April they were involved in defence of the Nieppe forest and fought on the Nieppe front between May and August, before fighting in the Battle of Bapaume.

They then went into action against the Hindenburg line in the following month before advancing to the Selle where they again fought during the final throes of the war. They completed their action in the battle at Sambre in November, and returned to England in April 1919.

It is perhaps surprising just how much travelling the soldiers did, and the number of theatres of war they were involved in. It is equally amazing that some previously untrained soldiers survived the whole of this campaign uninjured and returned to 'civvy street' after The Armistice.

- **9th Battalion Devon Regiment**

The 9th were formed at Exeter on 15 September 1914 as part of K2 and attached as Divisional Troops to 20th (Light) Division. In April 1915 it left Division and landed at Le Havre on the 28 July 1915 where it joined the 20th Brigade of the 7th Division.

Both regiments moved south of la Bassee canal on 24 September 1915. Their first big battle was the one at Loos, and after much heavy fighting and gas having been used their casualty list was 15 officers and 461 men. The 8th battalion who had accompanied them also suffered the heavy loss of 19 officers and 148 other ranks killed, 129 missing, with 343 suffering from the effects of gas and other wounds. They then proceeded to the Somme to join the other 615 Divisions who fought there. They were assigned to the Fricourt sector and served there until June.

Exeter Cathedral – Bronze War Memorial to the Men of Devon.

TO THE GLORY OF GOD ✠ IN MEMORY OF THE OFFICERS WARRANT OFFICERS N C OFFICERS ✠ MEN OF THE DEVONSHIRE REGIMENT WHO LOST THEIR LIVES DURING THE WAR 1914-1919

The prophecies of Captain D.L. Martin of the 9th Regiment that a machine gun hidden in a shrine in Mametz Cemetery would inflict heavy casualties on his Battalion is one of the many stories told of the Battle of the Somme. It is reported that whilst home on leave, just prior to the attack, he made a model of the area to be attacked by the Devon's. When they subsequently did attack through Mansell Copse, the weapon situated exactly where the officer had said was to account for many of the Battalion's losses, Captain Martin being one of the first to fall.

They were then involved in operations on the Somme attack on High Wood in July 1916, in the next two months at Mametz, and at Ginchy in September. They again suffered heavy casualties.

The Battalion moved to the Lys valley in November and on to operations in the Beaumont Hamel sector from December 1916 until the following March before heading to the Hindenburg Line. They then attacked Ecoust and Bullecourt, and it was at this time that William Beer was killed in action.

Their next move was to Belgium on August 17 and they were involved in the attack on Ghelvuett, again suffering numerous casualties there prior to a move to Italy to the Piave front in the spring of 1918. They returned to France in September, and joined the 20th Division attack at Beaurevoir in October.

They did not return to England until June 1919.

Additional material on these regiments kindly provided by Brian Burrows.

- **10th (Service) Battalion**

This battalion was formed at Exeter on 25 September 1914 as part of K3, coming under orders of 79th Brigade, 26th Division.

On 23 September 1915 it landed at Boulogne, and in November 1915 was moved with the Division to Salonika.

- **11th (Reserve) Battalion**

This battalion was formed in Exeter in November 1914 as a Service battalion, part of K4. In November 1914 it came under orders of 100th Brigade, original 33rd Division. Then on 10 April 1915 it became a Reserve battalion. Service battalions were responsible for getting food, ammunition and other supplies to the necessary theatres of war. On 1st September 1916 it converted into 44th Training Reserve Battalion in 10th Reserve Brigade.

- **12th (Labour) Battalion**

The 12th was formed in Devonport in May 1916. It landed in France in June 1916 and joined to Fourth Army. April 1917 it transferred to Labour Corps as 152nd and 153rd Labour companies. William Pennington was a member of this corps.

The following table shows that at this time there was a detachment of the Hussars at Woolsery. With its great dependence on horses for its agriculture it is not surprising that some of the local boys joined this unit, and at least one took his own horse to war.

The Royal North Devon
Yeomanry which included the
Hussars

HQ	Barnstaple
A Squadron	Holsworthy (detachments at Black Torrington, Hatherleigh, Bratton Clovelly, Tavistock, Woodford Bridge, Bradworthy)
B Squadron	Barnstaple (detachments at Atherington, Bratton Fleming, Blackmoor Gate, Fremington, Swimbridge, West Down, Braunton)
C Squadron	South Molton (detachments at West Buckland, Molland, Chittlehampton, Sandyway, Ashreigney, Chulmleigh)
D Squadron	Torrington (detachments at **Woolsery**, Langtree, Parkham, High Bickington, Bideford, Roborough)

At the outbreak of the First World War, the regiment was part of the 2nd South Western Mounted Brigade. It mobilised on 4 August 1914 and, with its brigade, moved to the Colchester area. It was dismounted in September 1915. Still with the 2nd South Western Mounted Brigade, the regiment left Colchester for Liverpool. On 24 September it boarded RMS *Olympic* and sailed the next day. It arrived at Mudros on 1 October and on to Suvla Bay. The regiment landed in Gallipoli on 9 October and was attached to the 11th (Northern) Division. In November it was in the firing line, and on 19 December it was evacuated to Imbros. On 30 December 1915, the regiment landed in Alexandria to help defend Egypt. Two months later 2nd South Western Mounted Brigade was absorbed into the 2nd Dismounted Brigade. It served on Suez Canal defences and part of the Western Frontier Force. On 4 January 1917, the regiment was amalgamated with the 1/1st Royal 1st Devon Yeomanry at Moascar, Egypt to form the 16th (Royal 1st Devon and Royal North Devon Yeomanry) Battalion, Devonshire Regiment and 2nd Dismounted Brigade became 229th Brigade in the 74th (Yeomanry) Division. It took part in the invasion of Palestine in 1917 and 1918. It then fought in the Second and Third Battles of Gaza (including the capture of Beersheba and the Sheria Position).

At the end of 1917, it took part in the capture and defence of Jerusalem, and in March 1918 in the Battle of Tell 'Asur. On 3 April 1918, the Division was warned that it would move to France, and by 30 April 1918 had completed embarkation at Alexandria. On 7 May 1918, 16th (Royal 1st Devon and Royal North Devon Yeomanry) Battalion, Devonshire Regiment landed at Marseilles, France with 74th Yeomanry Division. It served in France and Flanders with the division for the rest of the war. From September 1918, as part of III Corps of Fourth Army, it took part in the Hundred Days Offensive including the Second Battle of the Somme (Second Battle of Bapaume) and the Battles of the Hindenburg Line (Battle of Épehy). In October and November 1918 it took part in the Final Advance in Artois and Flanders. By the Armistice it was east of Tournai, Belgium, still with 229th Brigade, 74th (Yeomanry).

These soldiers fought a long and hard war, and those who survived must have counted themselves very fortunate.

Some of the village heroes found themselves involved in the East African campaign which comprised of battles and guerrilla actions, which started in German East Africa and spread to portions of Mozambique, Northern Rhodesia, British East Africa, Uganda and the Belgian Congo. The campaign was effectively ended in November 1917. The Germans entered Portuguese East Africa and continued the campaign living off Portuguese supplies.

The strategy of the German colonial forces was to divert forces from the Western Front to Africa. This strategy achieved only mixed results after 1916, when they were driven out of German East Africa and Allied forces became composed almost entirely of South African, Indian, and other colonial troops. South African troops were not considered for European service as a matter of policy while all Indian units had been withdrawn from the Western Front by the end of 1915; the campaign in Africa consumed considerable amounts of money and war material that could have gone to other fronts The Germans fought for the whole of World War I, receiving word of the armistice on 14 November 1918 at 7:30 a.m. Both sides waited for confirmation and the Germans formally surrendered on 25 November. German East Africa became two League of Nations Class B Mandates, Tanganyika territory of the United Kingdom and Ruanda-Urundi of Belgium, while the Kionga Triangle became a mandate of Portugal. Dar-es-Salaam was in Tanganyika, now Tanzania.

British road makers like Royal Engineer Albert Collings were amongst those sent out in the later stages of the war, and afterwards, to repair and improve the infrastructure.

Woolsery in 1914

From this somewhat isolated village far away from major towns and with limited access to world affairs, one might wonder how well over fifty of its inhabitants went off to fight in those foreign fields. This book tells their story, as well as it can be told, from records available from that time.

The starting point for looking at the war heroes from any community of a hundred years ago is probably always going to be the war memorial. The one on the wall in All Hallows Church, Woolsery helpfully lists those who returned as well as those who laid down their lives.

The war memorial itself is not always an accurate account as some people seem to have been added to a community monument because they had a family connection rather than a residential, or even birth, tie to the village or town. Some were not added simply because no-one requested that they should be recorded. Others who suffered severe trauma from the theatre of war and were termed deserters, or worse, and punished accordingly were not recorded as the viewers of the *Downton Abbey* TV series will be aware. It is, however, certain that none of this village's soldiers were listed and shot as deserters. These poor souls were often shell shock and gas victims who barely knew they were deserting, and were only pardoned in 2008. 306 service men were shot at dawn for this crime, the youngest being just 16 years of age. Shell shock, caused all manner of mental disabilities and indeed caused crimes to be committed throughout the rest of some victims, and their family's lives.

Woolsery certainly did not appear to have an unemployment problem in the 1911 Census, but for some young men who had rarely left their parish, the opportunity to visit fields anew, sparked by the patriotic call to arms of local dignitaries and certainly their clergyman, may have enthused them to rush to sign up and defend their country.

The October 13th 1914 edition of the *Bideford Gazette* recalled that a well attended recruiting meeting had been held in the Parish Room on the previous Saturday by the Bideford District League. Mr. J. Harding presided and the urgent need for every able bodied young man to join his Majesty's forces at this critical time was ably put by C.S. Parks, W.T. Charlwood and J.S. Dymond. There was much enthusiasm as six young men; James Henry Cook, John Thomas Prouse, William Hocking, William Prouse, Albert J .Prance and Edwin Stacey presented themselves for enlistment.

It was hoped that their splendid example would be followed by other young men in the district. A hearty vote of thanks was accorded to the speakers on the motion of Reverend Burrough, seconded by Mr. P. Bond. The Parochial Council were thanked for the use of the room and hearty cheers were raised for the King and his new recruits.

The following year, Woolsery's own vicar, now in his 26th year as incumbent, who had seen two of his own sons enlist, wrote in his parish magazine that on the previous day, Wednesday 17th February, the parish was visited by a troop of some fifty soldiers of the Devon Regiment with their officers and band. "The object of their visit was to endeavour to interest our people in the serious aspects of the war and to obtain additional recruits for our army". He was requested to welcome the soldiers on behalf of the parish and to invite them to partake of some light refreshments provided for them in the Parish Room, adjacent to the churchyard. This had been decided upon by the Parish Council, and admirably provided by a committee of ladies hurriedly convened on the Monday evening. Special thanks were due to them, he wrote, to those who had set to work at such short notice to make the cakes and cut rounds. A large number of parishioners assembled to greet the soldiers in the open space outside the church. An introductory speech, described as nice, was made by Mr. Millman, who pointed out the great necessity to increase our army in order to meet our national needs. Out of our population of about 475, he said, it is not felt that Woolsery had sent its fair proportion of men only about twelve having gone. In 1911 there was no-one called Millman living in the parish, but there were three farmers of that name living in nearby Bradworthy and Sutcombe, so presumably it was one of them.

The vicar continued by writing that he appreciated the difficulties and home wants, but felt that more men should go. The recruits are wanted by all classes, not just the working classes. Farmer's sons should ask themselves "Can I be spared?" He had not held back his own son and thought others should be of a like mind. The national need was great and our very existence as an empire was at stake, our homes needed defending and our women and children protecting. He ended his words to potential volunteers by asking if we wanted to suffer the horrors that were and are being committed in Belgium, which had already been over-run. Stories of atrocities in that country by occupation troops were widespread.

The National Anthem was sung and cheers were raised for King and Army. The young lieutenant in command of the troops told Reverend Burrough that in all the villages he had visited not one crowd contained so many men who were fit to enlist as the one he saw in Woolsery, and yet not one had stepped forward to sign up and the fifty brave soldiers, every one of whom had come from the trenches in France, marched away feeling disheartened that in spite of a warm welcome, Woolsery did not practically help them.

It appears that the young lieutenant was marching his troop all around North Devon seeking enlistment. At one time he is mentioned as having his arm still in a sling from a wound received at the Battle of Bassee in Northern France during October 1914.

Whilst they were at Chittlehampton a young woman with three children was in the crowd. She was told that if her husband went to war she would receive thirty shillings per week to feed her infants and that she would not have to look after her "old man." It was reported that her face lit up at the prospect and she asked "Do you think it will last long?" It is not recorded whether he took the hint and enlisted.

It is not perhaps surprising that the medical officer for Northam later in 1915 reported that the birth rate was falling, and whereas he normally expected fifteen or sixteen births per month the number had fallen to just five.

The vicar wrote that he feared that conscription would be imminent if Englishmen did not volunteer, and thus the honour of fighting would be gone. And he hoped that "perhaps some of our young friends will think this over and bravely offer their services".

We do not know if his strong words had any effect, but certainly a great many local lads went to war either before or after conscription was introduced.

Tattersills Grocers of Bideford were proud to take out a large advert in the Gazette proclaiming that 14 of their employees, some 43% of their workforce, had gone to enrol. Only eight were accepted; the other six were presumably not of the required fitness and so returned to serve their customers.

It is a matter of conjecture as to whether Lord Kitchener's famous poster appeared on the church notice board and elsewhere in the village. When young men did turn up to enrol, birth certificates were not scrupulously inspected and if a volunteer said he was old enough …. if he was fit then he was old enough! More than one local teenager signed up prior to his eighteenth birthday.

Clearly, even in fairly remote villages the pressure to enlist was put upon all able bodied young men, and yet still conscription eventually became inevitable. Men must have been terribly split by the call of the nation and the responsibility of being at home for the needs of one's family.

Between these two Woolsery enrolment meetings a poem was copied by the Gazette from the *Daily Chronicle*, it began:

> Hold hard before you call us names
> We're not afraid to die
> We'll down our tools we'll quit our games
> We'll march until our feet are sore
> We'll stand until we're stunned
> But will you find two million more.

This is one of many patriotic poems published at that time, but it should be remembered that with the advent some thirty years earlier of compulsory schooling, these were the first generations of young men, the majority of whom would be able to read.

In 1915 the NFU in London was very concerned about enlistment for a different reason. It said that industrial workers were enrolling faster than farm labourers, but were anxious that the government targeted single men and were less forceful at getting the married ones to enrol. They said that shepherds, carters and cowmen were indispensable and could not be replaced, so they were more valuable on the land than in uniform.

At the same time the Board of Education stated that it was not necessary to take action in non-attendance cases if boys were urgently needed to work the farms. In individual cases, if the authorities were satisfied that no other labour was available, it should be permitted. In March, the county of Devon agreed that 13 year old boys could work without fear of anyone being prosecuted.

In January 1916, after conscription had been agreed by parliament, all single or childless widowed men aged between 18 and 41 were due to be enlisted compulsorily. It was further decreed on 2 March that all men in this category were deemed to be enlisted, or were to expect to be enlisted shortly. A few months prior to the end of the war conscription was extended to men over 41.

Not long afterwards the *Bideford Gazette* was reporting almost weekly on locally held exemption tribunals and the decisions made therein. Men who were due to be called up for military service were able to appeal against their conscription; they or their employers, could appeal to a local Military Service Tribunal. Many of those working in agriculture to feed the nation certainly had a *bona fide* reason to appeal, but were met with varying degrees of interpretation of their value at these hearings.

A variety of jobs were exempted if the business was threatened by the employee's departure, but this was not always recognised by the authorities. Exemptions were given, but usually only for short periods of two to six months so that a changing war situation could quickly cause even more to be enlisted.

A Mr. Pickard complained that of the 18 employees of his painting and decorating business, 11 had already gone and three more awaited their mobilisation dates. The employee in question was given a short term exemption to be reviewed in October. An Abbotsham farmer was told to seek employees from the over age group when he complained that all of his four farm workers were being extracted from his business.

R. Wickett, a farm hand from Woolsery, was exempted for five months as he was the only hand left on a farm. An Appledore appellant stated that he was a teacher at Bideford Grammar School and unmarried, but supporting his aged mother. His appeal had not been granted a fair hearing at Northam as Appledorians were not given one there so he had now come to Bideford for justice! He claimed his grounds were domestic and a loss of earnings. He was informed that he was a most undeserving case and that he was wasting the Tribunal's time; other people's sons were going to war and he too must be enlisted.

A Bideford shoemaker petitioned to be allowed to keep his son in the business as the other two had already gone to war. His application was denied.

A licensed victualler was also given short shrift, being told that his role was not vital for the nation's good.

Mr Roundsell, headmaster of Shebbear College, applied for exemption for one of his pupils named Oswald Job as he was only just eighteen and preparing for an entrance examination for London University. He was an intelligent young man and in all probability would become a teacher and the nation would need a great many of these when the war was over. He said that the farming class had not come off badly when it came to exemptions and so his pupil should be given the same consideration. A statement not likely to please local farmers whose families presumably provided many of his pupils. He was informed by the military representative that thousands of young men had left their studies to defend their freedom. Oswald was given four months exemption to complete his exam preparation. The head teacher then commented that those under nineteen only had to complete six months training prior to their birthday. He was then asked why he had bothered to apply, to which he retorted that he had hoped for a longer period of exemption.

It is apparent that the military were not taking the advice, in many cases, that agriculture should be exempted. An Abbotsham man was the minder of a steam thresher, which was necessary in serving many local farms, and no replacement for his skills was available at any price. He was denied, but the agricultural representative informed the tribunal that he would appeal to Barnstaple for this just cause. In June, many agricultural applications were dealt with producing mixed outcomes, but none were from Woolsery.

William Tucker was aged 38, a widower and the father of four young children. He was employed by twenty local farmers and was an expert in rabbit trapping. He was said to have snared 11,300 the previous year. If left to run and eat, these rabbits would have consumed the equivalent of a bushel of corn so his efforts were an integral necessity of rural life. He was granted an exemption.

John Frederick Eastman, a Woolsery farm worker, was given an exemption as was (Richard) Percy Thomas, a small holder and rabbit trapper, but only for one month before he would have to apply again. This is the Percy Thomas who was the oldest former pupil to attend the village school's centenary celebrations in 1979, and records show that he did eventually join the army.

Four other farmers and labourers were given exemption until the harvest had been brought successfully in.

As the war neared its conclusion the forces were still desperate for manpower and when the bill was passed allowing men in their forties to be conscripted, agricultural workers were among those exempt. Men well into their forties were now appearing before tribunals requesting exemption, these were men who previously had thought themselves unlikely to be conscripted. At the same time the military lawyers were still battling for previously exempted young men, a young villager, William Prouse, aged 22, had previously been passed at C2 but they appealed successfully for him to be reassessed, and as the records show he eventually was called to arms. He had claimed that his agricultural work should exempt him.

Another William Prouse and village resident was a 33 year old skilled quarryman and blaster who was given a three month exemption when the County Surveyor explained that it was unfair that tree men were exempt but men who kept the roads passable were not.

He too eventually ended up in the army.

At the commencement of the Great War, Queen Victoria's grandson King George V was the monarch as his nation was preparing to fight against another grandson, Kaiser Wilhelm. This caused George to change his royal house name from Saxe-Coburg and Gotha to the less Germanic Windsor. His two elder sons, both future kings - Edward VIII and George VI - served in the war. Tsar Nicholas II of Russia, who was assassinated shortly before the end of the conflict, was also a grandson of Victoria.

The West End in London was enjoying the first performances of George Bernard Shaw's *Pygmalion* which forty two years later became the musical *My Fair Lady*. It is highly unlikely that anyone from this village made the journey to see the play at that time. Blackburn Rovers won the F.A. Cup, Johnny Douglas had resumed the England cricket captaincy from super sportsman C. B. Fry, and a pint of beer was "tuppence hapenny", or one new penny. Dinner at the Savoy would have cost you seven shillings and sixpence (37.5p) and Herbert Asquith, the prime minister was on £5,000 per annum. In 1914 the average wage for a basic 58 hours working week was 16 shillings and 9 pence.

You could have gone to Bideford, with half a crown (12.5p), on the omnibus, bought a large loaf, a pint of milk, a quarter of tea, a pound of sirloin beef, 6 eggs and a pound of sugar and still had a penny left for your fare home. A farm labourer would have to work more than half a day to earn that half crown. The pound of 1914 was only worth 2p in 1994 and even less today. Farley's Grocers, 82 High Street, Bideford were advertising bacon for nine pence halfpenny and pre-Shrove Tuesday were offering pancake flour at "tuppence hapenny" (1p) per bag, which would make lovely pancakes without the need to add eggs. Elsewhere you could purchase a dozen bottles of oatmeal stout for half a crown (12.5p). G. Boyle's, also in the High Street, would sell you a Raleigh bicycle for five pounds nineteen shillings and sixpence, or if you preferred hire purchase, nine shillings and four pence a month, but fails to disclose the length of the so-called hire period.

A Maxwell car from Heard's Garages on Broad Quay in Bideford - there is now a small supermarket on the site beneath the copper dome - would have cost £125. You may have preferred to go to Barnstaple to the County Garage in the square where £230 would have bought you a 1913 Studebaker 20/25 horse powered former demonstration vehicle, which would have cost you £320 new. It had an electric lighting outfit, five to seven seats and self-starter; no winding that starter handle and risking a broken wrist. The car was a dark blue open version and no doubt very smart. That year the 20 miles per hour maximum speed limit was passed into law. John Andrew, the shopkeeper at Woolsery, was among the first to become motorised in this corner of North Devon. C.J. told me how his father sometimes took the schoolmaster and his wife out in the car.

Horse-drawn power was much more the order of the day. William Lee of Ivy Cottage owned a four-in-hand wagonette for which he had failed to pay his licence fee. This was obviously a rather grand vehicle as the vast majority of horse-drawn vehicles had one or at most two animals to pull it along. He was caught returning from a day out at Bucks Mills with his wife and three children by a local constable, and he claimed that it was a market vehicle or cart which the magistrates were informed it was clearly not. He had paid tax the previous year but had failed to do so for 1914. He was found guilty and fined a total of fifteen shillings, but as he could have been required to pay £20 was deemed to get off lightly. He did not consider this generous and stated that he would rather go to prison, but was informed that this was not an option and that the money would be forcibly taken if necessary; with that the fine was duly paid. He was recorded as a blacksmith in 1901 and as a farmer ten years later.

The Gazette of those days contained many interesting advertisements on its front page including several 'wonder cures' which you could buy for all manner of ailments. It's amazing how so many people died prematurely if the adverts were all telling the truth. Dr Cassell's tablets would quickly solve the problems you might be having with acute bowel consumption among other diseases. You could have visited Mr Lionel Davis at 32 Lime Grove to get a tooth painlessly extracted for one shilling, or bought a set of artificial teeth for £2 a set, quite a substantial amount at that time.

Old Scotch whisky was on sale in Bideford for three shillings and sixpence, and a new piano could be obtained for prices starting at £14.

In 1917 you could have gone to the Palace Theatre in Bideford to enjoy the two reel Charlie Chaplin film entitled 'Charlie the Heart Thief' as well as the usual supporting programme, which included the ninth weekly instalment of *Peg of the Ring*. Cinemas in those days, and indeed for many years later through - and after - the Second World War, showed weekly serials to try to ensure loyalty and regular visits by their patrons. 'Peg' was an American drama serial made in1916 and today all copies are deemed to have been lost.

As the war rolled on, adverts were posted for residents to arrange for cigarettes to be sent to their loved ones in uniform. 500 Players would cost eight shillings and sixpence delivered, and 1,000 Woodbines could be sent for only a few pence more.

The following advert was used to persuade customers to avail themselves of this service direct from factory to soldier:

> " There aint no shops to shop in
> There aint no grand hotels
> When you spend your days in dug-outs
> Doing 'olesale trade in shells."

Woolsery was still very much a farming village when the war commenced, and a very large majority of its men and many women were employed in agriculture or affiliated trades.

In 1901, 648 residents were recorded in the Census, falling to 629 ten years later. This is somewhat higher than the figures mentioned earlier by Rev. Burrough, but almost certainly included the people of Bucks who had their own priest at that time and so were not of his flock. The corresponding figures for Hartland were 1,634 falling to 1,570, Bideford 8,754 rising to 9,078, and Barnstaple 14,137 to 14,483. A slow movement from rural areas to towns can clearly be seen from these figures, although Clovelly went up by two people to 623 and has a very similar number today.

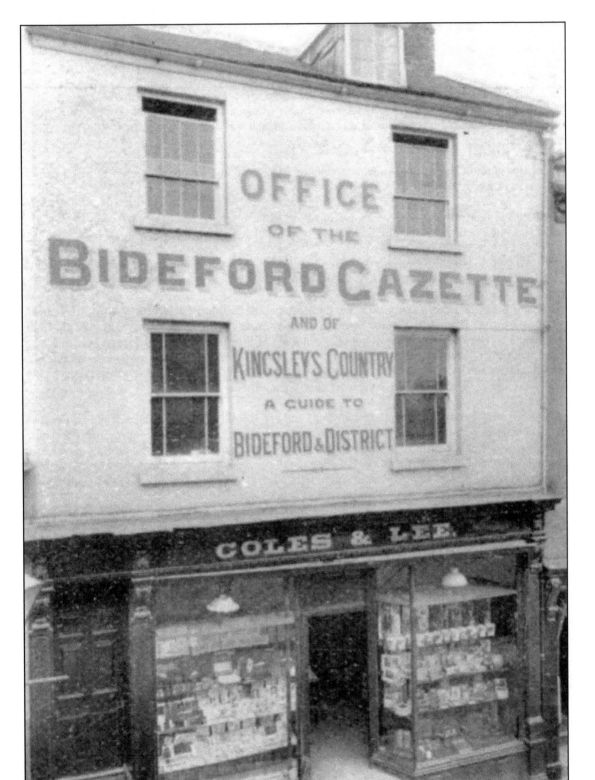

Most recent figures put Woolsery at 1,123, Hartland 910, Bideford 17,107, and Barnstaple 23,170 (2011).

In Woolsery the largest landowners around that time were Mrs. W.W. Melhuish of Court Barn Holsworthy, Mrs. Hamlyn at Clovelly Court, Richard James Cary Elwes of Walland Cary and William Wakeley of Alwington. It is noticeable that most of the land was owned by non-residents of the village and parish.

There was an omnibus, a horse-drawn vehicle, to Bideford daily, except at weekends, and a carrier twice a week run by Wm Burrow and A.P.Oke.

The parish contained 6,113 acres of land, 6 of water, 83 of foreshore, and of the 629 people recorded , 495 lived in the ecclesiastical parish.

Principal farmers were Richard Short, Thomas Cann, John Corey, Joseph Burrow, Job Sanders, John C Bond, Job Andrew and Thomas D. Burrow (who died in 1914).

Thirty people were listed as farmers in the directory published shortly before 1914; there were seven yeomen, which at this time meant they were freeholders of land, which they farmed. Other occupations included a hotelier, a cattle dealer, two millers, at Lane Mill and Leworthy, there was a boot maker, a blacksmith, four carpenters and a grocer/draper (who also farmed), at least two dress makers, two rabbit trappers and a rabbit dealer, an insurance agent, a telegraph wireman, a merchant, a stone breaker and four masons. Main crops were said to be oats, roots and wheat.

Within the village lived a variety of people young and old, the oldest being 90 and a retired farmer. The hotel contained its proprietor or manager, his wife, three daughters one of whom was a bar assistant, a carpenter who was a boarder, a servant, and another boarder who was one of several farm workers in the neighbourhood labelled as horsemen, working with horses or as teamsters, amusingly and wrongly translated as "tea maker" by one Census interpreter. Both of the hotel's boarders subsequently served in the army.

In July 1915 the Gazette reported a sale at Ashmansworthy on behalf of Mr Cory, which saw stock and grass sold off. Among the lots were three calves, which sold for between four and five pounds each. Cows in calf fetched £18 to £25 a head, and grass was sold for £3 an acre.

Other interesting stories from that paper included sad tales of an elderly lady, Mrs Nancekivell, being killed by a train at Westward Ho! Station, a little girl who died of burns, her coffin being carried to the grave by six choir boys, and a drowning at Abbotsham Cliffs.

The 1911 Census demanded that householders recorded the number of rooms in the dwelling, including the kitchen but excluding scullery, bathroom, landing, lobby, nor closet, warehouse or office. Toilet facilities were almost always outside of the main house and possibly shared with other homes. Researching those living in homes whose designated address is simply "The village" throws up some interesting data.

One four-roomed village house contained a man and his wife, and eight children. This family was typical of the majority, who had many children, 13 being the largest family recorded in the parish, all of whom survived childhood. Another four-roomed village home contained a married couple, their three sons, their daughter and her husband and baby son. Three of the four young men in that household went off to war. Some homes contained just three rooms!

It is interesting to note that of the married couples within the village, very few contained people who were both born here.

They included 2 couples born in Woolsery and Buckland Brewer, 1 Parkham and Meeth, 1 Woolsery and Fremington, 1 Stratton and Pyeworthy, 3 couples Woolsery and Clovelly, 1 Ashreigney and Woolsery, 1 Parkham and Clovelly, 1 Clovelly and Hartland, 1 Bridgerule and Hartland, 1 Tintagel and Woolsery, whilst only two were both born in the parish. It is clear that people moved around both to find work and a life partner.

Frederick Courtenay Burrough was the vicar, who was previously quoted, and he was to eventually see two of his sons go off to war. Both eventually returned home, although one had suffered severe leg injuries. A third son was Rev. Howard C Burrough who was visiting clergyman in the parish on a Sunday in May when he preached the sermon and spoke at a meeting on the lawn on the following Wednesday evening.

The vicar was born in Totnes and had worked in Wiltshire prior to taking the living and moving to the Cranford Vicarage. He resided there with his Irish second wife, some twenty years his junior, his first one having died, and children from his first marriage. The Woolfardisworthy College based in buildings at the vicarage had closed with the departure of the previous incumbent, Rev. William Holderness.

The vicar's magazine noted the improvement in the congregation on Sunday evenings but hoped that "those who could do would come in the morning, as well, as the whole day was the Lord's Day and the more we honour Him the more He will honour us and the blessing will be ours." Clearly farming and other interests were taking priority over morning attendance.

He enjoyed a reputation as being a caring, but pulpit-thumping, gentleman who had presided over the village since 1882, playing his role in civil as well as ecclesiastical matters. In his earlier quoted magazine of March 1915 he was disgusted that a neighbouring village had organised a whist drive and a dance to raise funds for Belgian refugees. He thought that local people should give freely to these poor unfortunates without the need to be entertained! It is easy, he wrote, to excuse frivolity under a veil of charity, but so thin a veil is easily seen through and the love of pleasure is clearly apparent. He hoped his own parishioners would see the unfitness of such things and set their faces against them. He realised that some thought him narrow minded, but he was strongly against this kind of amusement and clearly thought the church had no part in such goings on.

He took a lead as chair of school managers, forerunners of governors, in requesting the resignation of the previous headmaster and his wife due to their predilection for the bottle. Muriel Johns told me that it was rumoured that Mrs. Hicks always carried a reviver in her copious skirt and the records show that although the master was a diligent teacher who had taught well and introduced "continuation classes" (the forerunner of night school) he was accused of too often crossing the school yard to the pub in the evening.

The school was of course a county, not church, one but he still felt he had an important leadership role, which was gradually being diminished by the growing literacy among his congregation, not to mention the rise in popularity of the two non-conformist chapels within the parish.

Another copy of his Parish Magazine, this one for June 1914, which was two typewritten sheets in those days. The majority of it is taken up with obituaries to two men, Mr William Beer, "a dear old venerable figure who will long linger in our memories" aged 83. He had worked for the Burrow family at Lower Town farm for over forty years. "His time had come". For a year or two he had been failing and he contracted a chill while doing a little gardening on 17th April. Bronchitis and pneumonia set in and he passed away on the 27th.

The second was Mr Thomas Davey Burrow of Higher Town. He had been aged 79 years. He was one of several brothers well respected in Woolsery. "He had suffered from indifferent health a good deal, therefore his nervous system was considerably tried which resulted in a good deal of depression of mind which caused him to stay indoors."

Burrough reported that it had been his privilege to help the poor man to changes in his heart and feelings and to brighten at the promise of God and the hope which the Gospel brings. The vicar had stated that he had become greatly attached to the man and would miss him exceedingly. He went into further detail of the man's last days of coma and death.

It is clear that much greater detail of a person's afflictions were noted in the public obituary, and the language is also rather different from the written and spoken word of today.

The magazine goes on to report on a Scripture inspection of the school on March 20th. "The whole tone of the school has improved. A real spirit of reverence was manifest. The facts of the scriptures were well known. All the teachers are taking a deep interest in this work, with good results. The general work of the school is described in one comprehensive word EXCELLENT." He went on to congratulate Mr. Frederick Rogers and his wife "upon whom the responsibility rests", stating that "Religious Instruction is the foundation upon which character is built up. If that influences the heart, the lives will be right."

The Rogers had applied and been appointed to their posts after the exit of Mr and Mrs James Hicks from the school ten years earlier. The subsequent advertisement had been very clear about the God fearing, teetotal couple the managers were seeking and even suggested a man and his sister would be suitable. They lived in the school house, and he was born in Braunton and was aged 43 his wife Florence, born Torquay, was his assistant mistress, their two children Gwyneth and Ambrose had been born in Hastings where he was previously teaching. The Rogers were popular and stayed until 1930, when they retired. Mrs Rogers must have been very proud of two of her nephews; Dennis McCabe was awarded the military medal for bravery in 1917 and the Gazette reported that he was her second nephew to receive this very distinguished award.

Two lady inspectors had also recently visited the school and expressed their pleasure with the way that the needlework was done. This was of course only taught to the girls, whilst the boys followed more manly pursuits in those days far before the arrival of sexual equality.

The vicar had been appointed by the late Mrs. Hawkes who held that exalted position, but was never to be able to cast a vote as the suffragettes were only just escalating their protestations when she died.

The school, that year, accepted 25 new children, all born between 1899 and 1910. The new classroom, the one nearest the road, had been completed a few years earlier. At that time, the late Tom Peard informed me, he was an infant pupil there. Previously the youngest pupils had been taught in that small area just inside of the old school front door! The playground was still unpaved, the sign post was probably standing in it, and the back boundary of the school campus was the rear of the toilet block running through what would be the middle of the school library area today. The playing field was purchased some time later so that an area school could eventually be built there, closing some of its smaller neighbours. There was a well somewhere near the middle of what is now the rear classroom, but it was at that time adjacent to the house kitchen.

It can be seen how religious matters had a far larger influence on village life. The two other religious establishments in the parish were a Bible Christian Chapel and the Wesleyan one at Alminstone. The Bible Christian Church was a Methodist denomination founded by William O'Bryan, a Wesleyan Methodist local preacher, on 18 October 1815 in North Cornwall, with the first society, just 22 members, meeting at Lake Farm in Shebbear, Devon and was almost exclusive to the northern areas of the two counties.

The vicar had an income of approximately £200 per annum at that time and 16 acres of glebe land. Buckish St. Anne's also had its own vicar, who some years earlier was substantially better paid than the Woolsery one had been, as well as its own Church school. The late Raymond Heywood informed me that it closed shortly after the Second World War with no girls and just a handful of boys, of which he was one, on roll.

This, then, was the background from which these local heroes went off to war, many to face the horrors of trench warfare with the terror of German bullets to the fore, and the threat of a firing squad if they dared to take a backward step.

Firstly they had to face the drill yard and stern treatment by the regulars who were training them, and then they set off overseas. Those who went off to the European theatre of war found themselves in muddy trenches looking across fields of barbed wire and stakes, and suffering endless bombardments. The enemy was a hidden menace, who took away your friends or comrades with bullets and shells in a place where you witnessed unspeakable carnage and violent death. Others headed for the Middle East, like Thomas Johns who died in Palestine one week before the army drove the Turks out of Jerusalem.

Another, Thomas Rowe, served in Gallipoli and suffered severe frostbite before dying of enteric fever, more commonly known today as typhoid.

The most tragic family was undoubtedly the extended Beer family who, shortly after the school opened, lost three children, Arthur aged 8, Job aged 2 and Clara aged 12, to the terrible diphtheria epidemic which hit the area in 1879. They were three of seven who died in the village at that time. When war came, Private Job Beer was killed on the Western Front in 1918. Another Beer, William son of William and Tryphena of "Thornery", was a private in the Devonshire regiment who was also killed in action. His memorial is at Arras in the Fauberg D'Amiens Cemetery.

Another tragedy occurred after Archibald Stevens returned home from active service to get married to Miriam Cawsey from Worcestershire; he was a member of that county's Regiment. They married in Woolsery on Nov 17, and just twelve days later he lay dead on the battlefield in France.

At least two soldiers came home damaged by gas attacks in the trenches, and others who carried injuries for the rest of their lives, and who knows what other psychological damage the carnage they witnessed had wreaked upon them all.

Even as the war was reaching its end the vicar was involved in a correspondence with another resident of the area over what were seemly ways to raise money for the war effort. He was accused of being morose and a long faced Christian because he thought certain ways of raising cash were out of harmony with their objective. He believed in innocent recreation, but dancing and associated amusements don't afford pure and righteous enjoyment; they were in quite the opposite direction and militate against a spiritual religion as taught by our Lord. I am not quite sure what went on at dances during those years but he seemed to be under no illusion.

He even accused his critic as being un-Christian and in all probability a non-believer. Courtney Burrough was the chairman of a village war savings committee set up in 1917, which also included John Andrew - the shopkeeper - as the treasurer, Frank Rogers, the head master, was the secretary and Messrs Davey, Pennington and Burrow were the other members. In their first fortnight, 112 certificates for war bonds had been issued. He certainly thought this a more Christian way of raising funds.

He had begun that year by visiting every household in his scattered parish with copies of his Church magazine containing his New Year Address and motto. "Return unto me and I will return unto you with the Lord of heaven." A New Year parish tea was held with 200 residents in attendance and at 7.45 a service was held in the parish church for which the text of his sermon was his motto. He implored all denominations to turn to God in response to the clear call to war. "The singing was impressive", the Gazette also noted.

The British army (including troops from the British Empire) had 188,000 gas casualties but only 8,100 fatalities amongst them. In total there were about 1,250,000 gas casualties in the war but only 91,000 fatalities (less than 10%) with over 50% of these fatalities being Russian. However, these figures do not take into account the number of men who died from poison gas related injuries years after the end of the war; nor do they take into account the number of men who survived but were so badly incapacitated by poison gas that they could hold down no job once they had been released by the army.

You might experience some of the following symptoms after you inhaled or touched mustard gas: eye irritation, redness, burning, inflammation and even blindness. The skin became itchy and red but this was quickly replaced with yellow blisters. The respiratory system suffered runny or bloody nose, sneezing, hoarse throat, shortness of breath, coughing and/or sinus pain The digestive system could also be affected by abdominal pain, diarrhoea, fever, nausea and vomiting. Some of the more serious respiratory symptoms would take even longer to surface, needing anywhere from 24 to 48 hours to appear. This latent period played havoc with soldiers exposed during the war, rendering troops incapacitated, filling infirmaries, taking up valuable human resources, bogging down reinforcements and generally demoralizing soldiers.

Mustard gas can be lethal. But it doesn't kill quickly. Rather fatalities primarily result from secondary bronchial-pneumonia. Approximately 2 percent of all casualties who wore a respirator died from their injuries in World War I, compared to a death rate of 50 percent of those exposed without a respirator. The highest number of fatalities occurred after the third or fourth day of exposure, with the most extreme cases taking up to three to four weeks.

After an exposure to mustard gas, military doctors couldn't purge the effects of it in the body. Medical staff could treat the skin with ointments consisting of bleaching powder and white. Soldiers were left with respiratory and vocal problems and constant shakiness. I remember an elderly gentleman, a friend of my uncle's, who was suffering from these symptoms, when I was a boy in the fifties; a long time after the end of the Great War.

The following table shows the forces and casualties engaged in the conflict;

Country	Total Mobilized Forces	Killed	Wounded	Prisoners and Missing	Total Casualties	Casualties as % of Forces
ALLIED AND ASSOCIATED POWERS						
Russia	12,000,000	1,700,000	4,950,000	2,500,000	9,150,000	76.3
British Empire	8,904,467	908,371	2,090,212	191,652	3,190,235	35.8
France	8,410,000	1,357,800	4,266,000	537,000	6,160,800	73.3
Italy	5,615,000	650,000	947,000	600,000	2,197,000	39.1
United States	4,355,000	116,516	204,002	4,500	323,018	7.1
Japan	800,000	300	907	3	1,210	0.2
Romania	750,000	335,706	120,000	80,000	535,706	71.4
Serbia	707,343	45,000	133,148	152,958	331,106	46.8
Belgium	267,000	13,716	44,686	34,659	93,061	34.9
Greece	230,000	5,000	21,000	1,000	27,000	11.7
Portugal	100,000	7,222	13,751	12,318	33,291	33.3
Montenegro	50,000	3,000	10,000	7,000	20,000	40.0
TOTAL	**42,188,810**	**5,142,631**	**12,800,706**	**4,121,090**	**22,062,427**	**52.3**
ALLIED AND ASSOCIATED POWERS						
Germany	11,000,000	1,773,700	4,216,058	1,152,800	7,142,558	64.9
Austria-Hungary	7,800,000	1,200,000	3,620,000	2,200,000	7,020,000	90.0
Turkey	2,850,000	325,000	400,000	250,000	975,000	34.2
Bulgaria	1,200,000	87,500	152,390	27,029	266,919	22.2
TOTAL	**22,850,000**	**3,386,200**	**8,388,448**	**3,629,829**	**15,404,477**	**67.4**
GRAND TOTAL	**65,038,810**	**8,528,831**	**21,189,154**	**7,750,919**	**37,466,904**	**57.5**

Ordinary soldiers could be classed as shell-shocked or suffering post traumatic stress disorder even though it was not officially recognised until 1980. Many were locked up in local asylums with their problems blamed on hereditary or alcohol problems, whilst many others returned to their families taking their problems with them. Officers, however, were classed as suffering neurasthenia and were naturally nursed in more comfortable surroundings.

At least three served time in prison camps behind enemy lines but lived to return to their homes when hostilities concluded.

Some of those recorded were clearly very much men of the parish, others it is difficult to trace as having any links whatever when perusing school, war and census records. Searching for the men on the memorial for Woolsery throws up just one name for which it seems impossible to find any ties to the village, but perhaps his link will become more obvious when the 1921 Census is published, however current opinion is that it will not be released until it is almost a century old.

The facts recorded are, as always, a work in progress and no guarantee can be given of their accuracy but they are to the best of knowledge fairly accurate. Problems in research include the problem of when different spellings of the same name or address were recorded. School and census records also assist in piecing together the stories of these men but one can never be sure that everything is accurate, as some conjecture is always necessary when correlating information

One family gave their two sons two names each at birth and on the next census used one name and the following time their other Christian name. They clearly were not out to help historical research into them in future years.

The War ends

The time and date of the cease fire at the end of hostilities is probably one of the most famous in history and still remembered with sadness and pride each year. The *Hartland and West Country Chronicle* of 29 November 1918 records how the event was celebrated in the village.

"The glad news that the War was at an end reached Woolsery about noon, and was welcomed with every sign of joy and thankfulness. A flag was hoisted on the church tower and merry peals were rung as soon as the bell ringers could be gathered together. Flags soon decorated the village and the children did their best to enliven matters. The parish being a scattered one, it was not possible to arrange a service on that day.

A small meeting had been arranged in the evening among the Wesleyans at the Alminstone Chapel, the vicar and his household being glad to join in that service of Thanksgiving. A service was held in the Parish Church on Wednesday evening at 7.30 p.m. which was crowded by a most devout congregation and was conducted by the vicar, Rev. F. Courtney Burrough, who addressed it from the 103rd psalm verses 1 to 8. The service was joined in most heartily and the hymns were sung with beautiful fervour. It was an inspiring time, bells were rung and the parishioners wended their way homeward by the bright moonlight, not soon to forget the advent of the advent of the long prayed for peace."

Psalm 103

[1] Praise the LORD, my soul;
    all my inmost being, praise his holy name.
[2] Praise the LORD, my soul,
    and forget not all his benefits—
[3] who forgives all your sins
    and heals all your diseases,
[4] who redeems your life from the pit
    and crowns you with love and compassion,
[5] who satisfies your desires with good things
    so that your youth is renewed like the eagle's.
[6] The LORD works righteousness
    and justice for all the oppressed.
[7] He made known his ways to Moses,
    his deeds to the people of Israel:
[8] The LORD is compassionate and gracious,
    slow to anger, abounding in love.

The *Bideford Gazette* and the *Hartland Chronicle* shared the same correspondent, as the wording of their accounts of these events are exactly the same.

No mention is made of any celebratory parties, but perhaps the vicar would have frowned on that as he had on merry events being held to raise funds for the war effort as previously mentioned. Some families now looked forward to their loved ones returning, whilst others mourned the fact that theirs were for ever buried in a foreign field.

Contemporary local reports mention that various events were being cancelled due to the virulent flu epidemic, commonly remembered as Spanish flu, which had reached this area at that time. The virus killed 50 million people and attacked more than one-third of the world's population. Within months it had killed three times as many as the War had – and did it more quickly than any other illness in recorded history. 15-40 year-olds were the most susceptible, probably because they had not lived long enough to develop the immunities acquired during previous flu epidemics by members of older generations. Many soldiers returning, or awaiting their turn to head for home, were afflicted and a great number were killed by it having survived up to four years of carnage on the battlefields, leaving even more young women without a male partner to share their lives. A loving embrace exchanged at the end of the war between two people who may not have seen each other for several years risked the immediate transfer of the disease. The huge crowds that attended the Armistice celebrations in Trafalgar Square in London, and hundreds of communal spaces up and down the country intensified the chances of the disease spreading.

As one dangerous chapter ended, so another one was sadly beginning.

WHO'S ABSENT?

Is it You?

Albert Victor Andrew

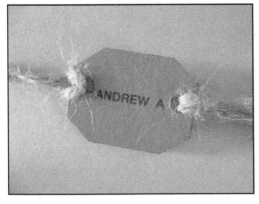

Albert was born in Woolsery in 1892, his parents were George and Norah Ann, née Moore, who were married two years earlier. His father was recorded as being a tailor and rabbit dealer in 1911 and they lived at Cranford Cottages.

His siblings were Thomas born 1894, Sidney William in1897 Matilda May three years later, Catherine Mary 1903, Gwendoline in 1905 and Lena Elizabeth the youngest was born in 1907. Albert was a farm worker who married Frances E. Daniels from Alwington in 1915. She was at that time a housemaid at Horns Cross and was born two years earlier than her husband. They had three children Welcome, who was born on Welcome Home Day which was 29th August 1919, Norah and Avril. Welcome married Vera Barriball in Launceston in 1944.

Little of Albert's war service is known other than he was in the army and features on the Woolsery war heroes photo having been identified as the 6th man from the left on the 2nd row from the back.

He has many relatives still living in the community at the time of writing in 2015, including Terry Harding who is his great great nephew, and he was the great uncle of Stuart Pennington and his sister Jill Piper. He was also the uncle of Stella Pennington and Bill and Eric Cann.

Cyril John (CJ) Andrew

Cyril Andrew, affectionately known in the village as CJ was born in Woolsery on 26th February 1899.

He attended the village school from 1904 until 1912. He once told me that his mother was reluctant to allow him to commence his studies until the head teacher and his wife had been asked to resign due to their liking for alcohol and had departed from the village. He transferred to Shebbear College in 1912 to complete his education.

He was the son of Anna and John, who ran the local shop, which was also a drapery and post office, but John was also recorded as a farmer and landowner.

Cyril's grandfather Job Andrew, was recorded as a farmer, tailor and shopkeeper. He was by 1911 a widower recorded as living with the family at the post office. The family were also one of the very first owners of a motor car in the area.

The shop, and their home, was where the village stores still

stands today. Their family was completed by Millicent born 1900, who in turn was the grandmother of Michael Birch, the entrepreneur who in 2015 bought the *Farmer's Arms,* the Woolsery Fish and Chip shop, and the *Manor House Hotel* intending to resurrect them from their derelict conditions.

CJ joined the Pioneer SIG. Company RE as Private 317158 and served in Palestine and Egypt. On completion of his war service he joined and eventually took over the family business.

The Post Office and shop was a thriving hub of village life employing several people and later delivered items by van around the community. The shop carried a vast and varied stock and sold petrol from the pumps outside.

He married Ida Cruse in 1922 and his descendants still live in the village at his old home, known as Fairholme. A well respected village resident and former parish councillor, he died on January 2nd 1990 aged 90.

Wilfred Andrew

Wilfred Andrew was born on the 16th May 1894 to Joseph and Mary Ann and attended Woolsery School. His parents farmed at Dipple where he was employed, and he eventually took over the farm before moving to another farm at Colins Down near Stibb Cross

The 1911 census records the marriage of Joseph and Mary Ann, née Moore, they produced eleven live births and all survived; something of a rarity in those times.

The other ten children were Ada born 1892, Hilda May 1896, Olive Mary 1897, Joseph 1899, Oswald 1900, Effie 1901, Mary 1903, Frank 1904, Aubrey 1902 and Dorothy (1910).

In 1921 he married Florrie Millman of Holsworthy.

Wilfred died in 1972 aged 78.

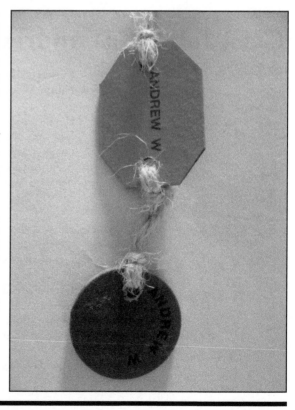

John Beckley

John Beckley was born in Woolsery in 1895 He did not attend Woolsery School, although both his sisters did.

His parents were William and Ann both of whom were born at Abbotsham, and his sisters, Florence born 1896 and Mary 1899. The family lived at Alminstone Cottages. John was a farm worker and married Minnie Squires in 1915.

He served as GNR 216165, 56th BTY 34th Bde Royal Field Artillery. He was the father of Percy Beckley of Pick Park, Woolsery and uncle of Bonham and Colin Jewell. John died in 1966 and was buried at Pancrasweek .

Arthur Beer

Arthur Beer was born in Woolsery on January 3rd 1894 and attended the village school from 1897 until 1907. He was the son of Francis Beer, a farm labourer, and Harriet Alice, née Prouse who lived at Church Park Cottage, which is now known as Copperhill.

Francis and Harriet had ten children: Job was born in 1877 and died in the diphtheria outbreak of 1879.

This was the year the school opened and the disease claimed the lives of at least seven children in the community. They then had Anna Marie (1879), Clara Jane born 1881, died 1884, Regina born 1883 died the following year, another Job 1886, who lost his life in the war, a second Clara Jane 1887, a second Regina 1890, Arthur 1894 (presumably named for his uncle who together with his sister Clara also died in the diphtheria outbreak of 1879), Francis Bertie (1897) and Gertrude (1898).

Arthur was a soldier and became a prisoner of war. He had a dream whilst resting on manoeuvres, about being captured and shortly afterwards he claimed it came to pass in exactly the way he had foreseen.. He also suffered the effects of gas in the trenches (WW1 gas attack pictured on previous page) which continued to affect him in later life.

On returning from prison camp he was a horseman at West Town Farm and later at Kennerland, and married Lucy who lived until 1989 aged 96. He was the uncle of Margaret Buckley.

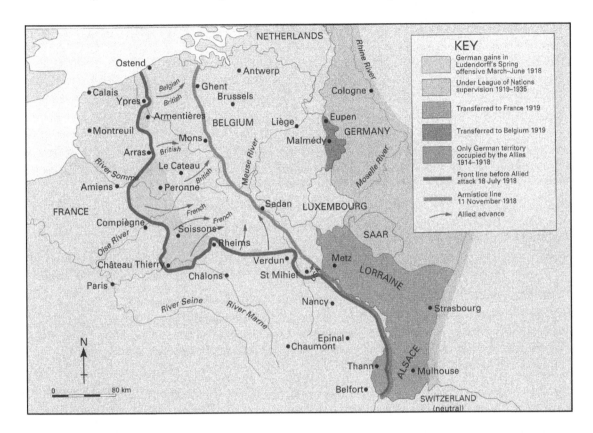

Job Beer

Job Beer was born in Woolsery on the 9th January 1886 and attended Woolsery School from 1889 until

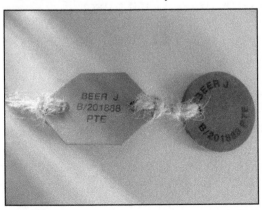

he left to go to work at the age of ten, which by then was not legally an option. He was the son of Francis Beer, a farm labourer, and Harriet Alice, née Prouse, who lived at Church Park Cottage now Copperhill, and the nephew of Arthur (above). As described above, Francis and Harriet had ten children.

Job was a farm labourer and was married to Sarah née Wonnacott They had three children Gertrude 11, Francis 9, and Lancelot 8 and a fourth Arthur who died aged 11 in 1923. They lived at 136 Dyke Green Clovelly (CWGC) He joined the army as Private 039668, enlisting at Exeter, then later became

Rifleman B/201888 1/28th Rifle Brigade (The Prince Consort's Own) and was killed on the 29th of March 1918 on the Western Front aged 32. He was fatally wounded in the fighting of the "Kaiser's Battle which began on 21st March.

The 1918 Kaiser's Battle or Spring Offensive, or also known as the Ludendorff Offensive, was a series of German attacks along the Western Front, beginning on 21 March 1918, which marked the deepest advances by either side since 1914.

The Germans had realised that their only remaining chance of victory was to defeat the Allies before the overwhelming human and other resources of the United States could be fully deployed. They also had the temporary advantage in numbers afforded by the nearly 50 divisions freed by the Russian surrender). There were four German offensives.

The one codenamed Michael was the main attack, which was intended to break through the Allied lines, outflank the British forces which held the front from the Somme River to the English Channel and

th Bn.
Feb.,
Ellen
usband
West

BECKWITH, Pte. George, 22371. 2nd/4th Bn. Duke of Wellington's Regt. 30th March, 1918. VI. G. 40.

CEMETERY Fr. 62 DOULLENS FRANCE EXTENSION I.

BEEBY, Pte. Herbert, 61465. 12th Bn. Manchester Regt. Died of wounds 27th April, 1918. Age 29. VI. A. 58.

41st
Age
arwell,

BEER, Pte. Job, B/201888. 1st Bn. Artists' Rifles. 29th March, 1918. Age 32. Husband of Sarah Beer, of 136, Dyke Green, Clovelly, North Devon. V. B. 11.

50603.
ounds
as and
. 45.

BELL, Rfn. Thomas Leslie, R/13594. 7th Bn. King's Royal Rifle Corps. 30th March, 1916. I. E. 4.

GV RI

Dieu et mon Droit

HE whom this scroll commemorates
was numbered among those who,
at the call of King and Country, left all
that was dear to them, endured hardness,
faced danger, and finally passed out of
the sight of men by the path of duty
and self-sacrifice, giving up their own
lives that others might live in freedom.
Let those who come after see to it
that his name be not forgotten.

Rifleman Job Be...
Rifle Brigade

defeat the British Army. Once this was achieved, it was hoped that the French would seek armistice terms. The other offensives were subsidiary to *Michael* and were designed to divert Allied forces from the main offensive on the Somme.

The Allies concentrated their main forces in the essential areas (the approaches to the Channel Ports and the rail junction of Amiens), while leaving strategically worthless ground, devastated by years of combat, lightly defended. The Germans were unable to move supplies and reinforcements fast enough to maintain their advance. The fast-moving storm troopers leading the attack could not carry enough food and ammunition to sustain themselves for long and all the German offensives petered out, largely through lack of supplies.

By late April 1918, the danger of a German breakthrough had passed. The German Army had suffered heavy casualties and now occupied ground of dubious value which would prove impossible to hold with such depleted units. It was repelling this vital attack that Job Beer gave his life. He was buried at Doullens Cemetery on the Somme. Doullens was the site of several Casualty Clearing Stations as well as a cemetery. A memorial service for the late rifleman Job Beer London Regiment Rifle Brigade who fell in action March 29th was reported to have taken place at All Saints Church, Clovelly. The Rector, the Reverend T.L. Simpkin, officiated.

The mourners present included Mrs Sarah Beer (widow) Master Francis Beer (son) Mr and Mrs Francis Beer, from Woolsery and presumably his parents, Mrs J. Foley , Mrs G. Babb (sisters-in-law, Mrs Wonnacott, Misses Bessie and Ethel Wonnacott, Mrs Headon, Mrs H. Prouse, Mrs W. Prouse and Mr D. Short. The list suggests a distinct lack of men folk due, no doubt, to so many being away at war. Sarah Stafford née Heard (Titchberry Farm) is his grand daughter, and Margaret Buckley his niece.

William Beer

William Beer was born in Woolfardisworthy on 25th August 1884.

His parents were William born Clovelly 1857 and his mother was Tryphena Beer, née Dell, also born in Woolfardisworthy 1854 and died there in 1910. The family lived at Thornworthy (Thornery) and then Back Street. He attended Woolsery School between 1890 and 1898.

In Memory of

Private

William Beer

25046, 9th Bn., Devonshire Regiment who died on 07 May 1917 Age 30

Son of William and Tryphena Beer, of Thornery, Clovelly, Devon; husband of Ellen Maud Beer, of Back St.,
Woolsery, Bucks Cross, Devon.

Remembered with Honour
Arras Memorial

Commemorated in perpetuity by

the Commonwealth War Graves Commission

He had six sisters; Mary Ann born 1881, Clara 1882, Tryphena born 1883 died 1884, Elsie 1891, Emily 1893 and Florence 1897. He worked as a farm worker and carter before joining the army, and married Ellen Maud Jeffery in 1906. He enlisted at Exeter as Private 25046 in the Devonshire Regiment 9th Service Battalion. He was killed in action on the Western Front 7/5/1917 and buried at Arras.

A stone in Woolsery Churchyard commemorates both William and his wife.

"William Beer who was killed in action in May 1917 aged 32 years also Ellen Maud beloved wife of above who died on 30th August 1944 aged 63". William was the cousin of Job and Arthur, his fellow soldiers. His home at that time was listed as Bucks.

The table below shows how the War and fatal infantile illness caused tragedy after tragedy for this unfortunate family.

BMD records show that other children with this surname, namely John Beer aged 0 in 1884, Hannah Beer also before her first birthday, Maud Mary, aged just one, as was Frances Alice, all three dying in 1885 and another Frances just a baby, in 1886 all died. I have been unable to ascertain which families they belonged to and indeed might be members of other Beer families in the wider Bideford area but their Christian names suggest that at least some were related to the branch in question. They were not the children of Francis as his 1911 census return indicates quite clearly that he had ten children and three were dead, Job becoming the fourth when he met his end in France. This clearly underlines the frequency and regularity of infant mortality at this time.

A family tree showing how war and fatal illness brought tragedy to the Beer family										
William born 1827 and Alice Beer born 1832 both at Clovelly										
Lived at Slade Cottage Clovelly (1861) and then West Town Woolsery (1871 and 1881)										
The children of William Beer and his wife Alice										
Mary Ann born 1851	Emily born 1853	Francis born 1855 Married Harriet Alice Prouse 1876 See below	William Born 1857 Married Tryphena 1878 See below	Thomas born 1859	John born 1861 Later an Ostler at Clovelly	Bessie born 1866	Clara born 1867 died in diptheria outbreak of 1879	Ernest born 1870 Had two children with Norah both died in infancy	Arthur born 1871 died in diptheria outbreak of 1879	Lily born 1874
The children of Francis Beer and his wife Harriet Alice nee Prouse										
Job born 1877 died in Diptheria outbreak of 1879	Anna Maria born 1879	Clara Jane born 1881 died 1884	Regina born 1883 died 1884	Job born 1886 killed in war 1917	Clara Jane the second born 1888	Regina the second born 1890	Arthur born 1894 went to war but survived	Francis Bertie born 1898	Gertude born 1899 Married Jim Cook In 1922	
The children of William Beer and his wife Tryphena nee Dell born 1854 Woolfardiworthy										
		Mary Ann born 1879	Clara born 1881	William born 1885 killed in France 1917		Tryphena born 1883 died 1884	Elsie born 1890	Emily born 1893	Florence born 1897	

William J. M. Bennett

William Bennett was born in Woolsery during 1882. His family appeared to move often and he attended school in Puddingon, which is in the Crediton area, as his parents moved there during his early years.

His father Richard, an agricultural labourer, was born at Washford Pyne and his mother Elizabeth was a Woolsery girl. William lived at Yowlestone Cottage, Puddington in 1891 but later the family returned to his father's birthplace.

Both worked as farm labourers, although Richard in 1911 was a dairyman on his own account and William was a carpenter. He had one sister, Eva, two years his senior and another sibling who seems impossible to find presumably being born and dying between census records.

A soldier named W. Bennett was reported missing from 8th Battalion Devon Regiment 2/11/15, but then found to be a prisoner of war on 14/2/1916

Was this him ??

George Brent

George Brent was born on 27th December 1896 and attended Woolsery School. He lived in the village, next door to George Goodenough the boot maker, with his parents Reuben a carpenter and wheelwright, and Ann née Glover, the family was completed by William Edward born 1885, who had tried to enlist but was declared medically unfit, Maria born 1889, John 1891 and George was the youngest.

In 1911 he was recorded as having just left school and not taken up employment, but later went into his father's trade. He was the great uncle of Marjorie Braund née Brent, who was school cook when I commenced my duties there, and to others including Norman, Clive and Ann Piper, Bill, Peter and Pauline Ashton. George suffered gas poisoning (A German gas attack from 1917 is pictured here courtesy Wikimedia Commons) whilst on

active service and was never really well on returning from the army. He died aged just 24. Perhaps he should be included amongst those who lost their lives in the war!

Frederick Stanley Burrough (Frank)

Frederick Burrough was born in Woolfardisworthy in 1894. His only school recorded is Blandford Grammar School where he was a student in 1911.

His parents were the Reverend Frederick Courtenay Burrough and his wife Alice, and his address was The Vicarage at Cranford. His siblings were Howard born in 1882, Alice in 1883, James, who also served, in 1884, Gertrude 1889 and Herbert 1891.

He was a member of the Gloucester Regiment in September 1916, and as a private was recorded to have got well within the German third line when a machine gun bullet passed through his left knee and partly through his right one causing him to be hospitalised. No record appears to be available for a marriage or his death suggesting he may have emigrated after the war.

James Walrond Burrough (Jim)

James W. Burrough was another child of the vicar Frederick Courtenay and Alice Burrough, living at Cranford Vicarage. He was born at Compton Chamberlaine in Wiltshire in 1884 where his father had previously been the incumbent.

He attended Blandford Grammar School and then went on to Bristol where in 1911 he was an engineering student. He later gained a B.Sc. His siblings were Howard born in 1882, Alice Louisa in 1883, Frederick, who also served, born in 1884, Gertrude 1889 and Herbert two years later. It is said that he was known locally as "Master Jim."

He was a Lieutenant in the Gloucester Regiment and on 21st September 1916 was shot through his left leg and injured also in the right one when well within the third line of German troops. Reported missing possibly a prisoner of war 24th October 1918, but must have safely returned eventually or his name would have been recorded amongst the war dead. He, like his brother, has no record in the marriages or deaths records.

William Cann

William Cann was born in Woolsery 29th January 1893 and attended Woolsery School. His parents were Charles and Alice, née Petherick, who farmed at South Stroxworthy, which had previously been farmed by Alice's father Daniel.

Alice had nine children. All survived, they were Susan born in 1878, Thomas 1882, Daniel 1884, Alice 1886, Charles 1888, Flossie 1891, John 1892, Florrie 1892 who was William's twin sister. William worked on the family farm before going to war.

He was Corporal machine gunner 663551 in the 51st Battery

William was the father of Bill Cann of Solitude, Parkham and uncle of Ida Cann of Stroxworthy, Florrie's daughter.

William, who had been affected by mustard gas during the war, died of diabetes complications in January 1938 aged just 44. He is pictured at the top of this page with his wife, and with Alfie Thorne, and his wartime medals are pictured on the following page.

James (Jim) Cook

Jim was born at Alwington in 1897. He would have attended school at Parkham or possibly Halwell, the former school on the main road near to *Hoops Inn*.

His parents were James born at Parkham in 1871, a horseman on a farm, and Eliza who was born at Alwington in 1868. They lived firstly at Ford Cottage Alwington and then at Sloo, Parkham

The family had 8 children who all survived in 1911, they were Lucy born in 1893, George Wm 1894, John Veale 1896 James Henry 1897 Mary Veale 1902, Ellen Hannah 1905, Emily Wilmot 1907.

Jim worked as a farm labourer at Howley Park, Parkham for Thomas Heddon and later lived at Forestry Cottage, Powler's Piece. He signed up aged just 17, lying that he was 18, and served in the trenches where he contracted diphtheria and amazingly survived, recovering in a field hospital to return to the front. Diptheria was a disease that killed well over 30% of its victims and often the younger ones. In 1922 he married Gertrude Beer, sister of Job and Arthur who also served. He was Margaret Buckley's father.

Eli Charles Cornish

Eli Charles Cornish proved elusive to research largely because his parents and their family moved around so much. He was the grandson of Philip and Ann Cornish of Kilkhampton and the son of Thomas William Cornish, a cattleman, also born there, and of Mary Ann, née Pennington, who was born in Hartland. His maternal grandmother, Grace, was from Woolfardisworthy. A tenuous link but the only one found to date. Perhaps Eli settled in Woolsery after the war.

The fact that he is recorded on the church wall as E.C. rather than his Christian names is curious and suggests he was not well known. Thomas and Mary had eleven children, of which nine were alive in

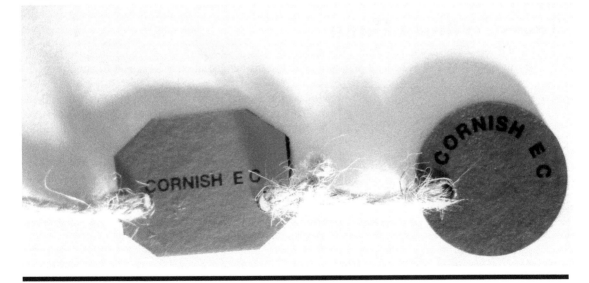

1911, Eli was the youngest of the survivors born in 1899.

The family at different times lived at Billacott North Petherwin, where Eli was born, Bradworthy where Edmund, one of his brothers was born, Bratton Clovelly, the birthplace of Nortram, an unusual name, Kilkhampton where William was born, Morwenstow the birthplace of Alfred, a traction engine driver, and Harold. Thomas and Albert were born at Poughill. Eli joined the Devon Regiment having still been a scholar when the last available census was made.

He became Private 345892. On the wounded and killed list of 10th January 1918 one soldier of the Devons had been killed, but countless others received wounds including one E. Cornish. The Gazette reported that he had been shot in the leg and face. It appears that he had returned on leave in 1917 and married Dorothy Daniel, a scullery maid at Portledge, and records show that Alberta born in 1918 and Eric 1922 may have been among their offspring.

Seth Davey

Seth Davey was born in Holsworthy on 28th August 1897 and attended   school there before moving to Lane Mill and attending Woolsery School. His parents were George Thomas Davey and Susan Davey, who was born in Worcestershire. Thomas is recorded in 1891 as being his father's assistant at Lane Mill before becoming a carpenter and grocer at Haytown in 190, then in 1911 had returned as miller having taken over from his father. George and Susan had seven children, the others being Huldah born in 1896, Melinda 1900, George T. 1901, Winifred 1903, Catherine 1906 and Cyril in 1910.

Seth is recorded as working as the miller's son in 1911. His grandfather, the miller was also called George Davey who had a son "the other Seth Davey" who was Ted Lott's grandfather. There is no record available of his war service.

Ernest William Dunn

Ernest Dunn was born on January 21st 1898 at Kesmeldon , West Putford where he attended school, until he was twelve, as well as being a regular member of the congregation at Sessacott Chapel.

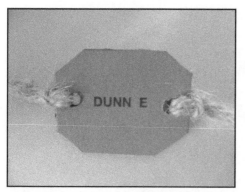

He was the second child of fourteen, three of whom died in infancy, and the family moved to Ashcroft, Woolsery in 1917. His parents were William, who was born in Abbotsham and Mary Jane who had been born at East Down; they were married in 1896. William had worked on his father Richard's farm there but then became a quarry delver for the council before returning to farming. William and Mary Jane are buried at Woolsery and his parents at West Putford, where the family are recorded to have lived as far back as 1650.

Standing L-R: Ernest, Stanley, Evelyn, Mildred, Harold, Arthur. Seated L-R: Ethel William Mary (holding Miriam), Annie. On Ground: Edgar, Elsie.

Other children of the marriage included Eliza who was born in 1897, Ethell Mary in 1900, Arthur John the following year, Mabel Annie in1904, Stanley Edward in 1907, Evelyn Florence in 1909 and Harold James who was a year younger. The 1911 Census records that there were eight births and all had survived, of the six subsequent births only three survived infancy.

The younger children attended Woolsery School. Ernest has no occupation recorded as he was still a pupil in 1911. He joined the army in 1918 and served until 1921.

Ernie married Melinda Davey, the sister of Seth Davey above at Alminstone Chapel on 8th March 1923. His parents had now moved to Higher Bradley Farm, Sheepwash and he lived and worked there until shortly after his daughter, Mary, was born. In early 1925 they moved to Seldon Farm Monkokehampton where their other five children were born. They were Melinda Mary, known as Mary b.5 Feb 1924, m. Norman Tancock, d. Feb 1973, William George, known as George, b.16 Jun 1925, m. Marion Goss, d.21 Mar 2009. Aubrey Ernest b.26 Apr 1927, m.

Mary (actually Joyce Mary) Holwill and currently lives at Cheriton Fitzpaine, Ivy May b.25 Jan 1929, m. Owen Holwill (brother of Joyce Mary) lives at Henacroft Farm, Iddesleigh, Cyril John, father of Roger, b.7 Feb 1930, m. Margaret Lock, d.22 Jul 2013 and Sylvia Christine b.12 Dec 1934, m. Reginald Anstey, d.28 Nov 2010.

On 25th March 1942 the family moved to Brimblecombe Farm, Iddesleigh.

He had become a Methodist preacher upon his return from the war in 1921 and continued until his sudden death in 1961 aged 63, when his widow was presented with a long service certificate awarded to him posthumously.

He was buried at Iddesleigh Methodist chapel where Melinda was also laid to rest, in 1994, some 33 years later aged 94.

Roger Dunn, his grandson, has provided additional information for this entry: I have attached a photo of the Dunn family, (page 79) which from the age of Miriam must have been taken around 1922, therefore quite likely at Ashcroft Farm. I wonder if anyone could take a photo of the location today, if it still exists and send this along as a comparison. Chances are that this area may have been incorporated into some kind of extension by now.

Family details:

1. Eliza Mildred b.6 Jan 1897, m. John A Sleeman, d.14 Jan 1949 Withybrook Farm, Sticklepath.
2. Ernest William b.21 Jan 1898, m. Melinda Davey, d.21 Apr 1961 Brimblecombe Farm, Iddesleigh.
3. Ethel Mary b.25 May 1899, m. Fred Prouse 10 Aug 1929 at Kilkhampton Wesleyan chapel. No further details.
4. Arthur John b.18 Mar 1901, m. Alice Maud Stevens, d.20 Mar 1972 Heath Farm, Bradworthy.
5. Mabel Annie b.15 Mar 1904, m. Frederick W Metherel, d.30 Mar 1946 Eddistone Farm, Hartland.
6. Stanley Edward b.21 Aug 1906, m. Beatrice Evelyn Cottle, d.5 May 1943 Berry Farm, Petrockstowe.
7. Evelyn Florence b.10 Aug 1908, m. Albert Jones, d.11 Feb 1967 West Putford.
8. Harold James b.20 Jun 1910, m. Elizabeth Catherine (Katie) Hockridge, d. ?
9. Elsie Margaret b. 24 Jun 1913, m. Frederick Robert Richards, d.24 Feb 1984 Hatherleigh.
10. Edgar George b.23 Dec 1915, m. Helena Jones (sister of Edward), d.30 Mar 1984 Alverdiscott.
11. Muriel Jane b.22 Jan 1917, d. 22 Jan 1917.*
12. Cyril Frederick b.9 May 1918, d.11 May 1918.*
13. Miriam Joyce b.15 Jun 1919, m. Edward Jones (brother of Helena), d.19 Nov 2003 Hatherleigh.
14. Unnamed b.30 Dec 1921, d.30 Dec 1921.*

* the 3 who died in infancy were unknown to the rest of the family until not long ago when a recipe book belonging to Mary Jane came to light in which she had written details of all her children, and if you think that the fact that infant mortality was common in that era made it easier to bear, then reading the few lines she wrote about those who didn't make it will make you think differently.

Of all the above named people only Edward Jones is still alive. He carved his and Miriam's initials in Hawkers hut the day before WW2 was declared. These initials can still be seen.

I have no stories about Ernie's time in the war, other than that it was on the battlefield that he found God and made the promise in a prayer to preach the gospel for the rest of his days. He, like so many others, didn't have a lot to say about his experiences.

Roger also sent another photo, reproduced here. He writes: "here you have their entire family. Standing L-R: Aubrey, Cyril, Mary, George, Ivy Seated L-R: Melinda, Sylvia, Ernest".

This photo was taken at Brimblecombe. Not certain of the year, but assuming Sylvia looks to be about 15 that would make it around 1949/50.

Frederick (Fred) Eastman

Frederick Eastman was born in High Bickington in 1891and attended school there. His parents were James, who was also born in High Bickington, and Elizabeth Annie who was from Torrington. They moved to Marshall Gate in 1910. James was a farmer at both places and Frederick worked for his father in 1911.

Fred had five brothers and sisters; William who was born in 1883, John in 1886, Henry 1893, Annie 1897, and one who had died in infancy. No record has been found of his war service, or indeed his later life, making no appearance in the marriage or death records. His brother also served as below.

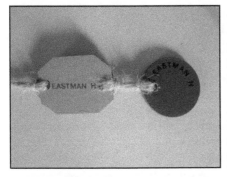

Henry (Harry) Eastman

Henry was born in High Bickington where he attended school. He is recorded as Henry in the 1901 Census but by 1911 is Harry.

His parents were James, who was also born in High Bickington, and Elizabeth who was from Torrington. They moved to Marshall Gate in 1910. James farmed at both places and Harry worked for his father in 1911. His siblings were William born in 1883, John in 1886, Frederick 1891, Annie 1897 and one who was recorded as deceased in 1911. No record has been found of his war service, or indeed his later life, making no appearance in the marriage or death records.

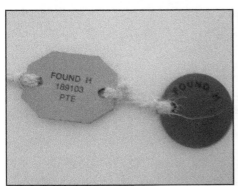

Henry (Harry) Found

Henry or Harry was born in Woolsery on 25th July 1904 but left the village three months after commencing his studies at the village school. The family had moved to Bideford, but returned to the village in 1910 and later lived at Cranford. His parents were Henry, a general haulier, who was born in Clovelly and Florence his mother who had been born in London. They lived at Venn Cottage with their three other children, Beatrice born in 1905, William in 1911 and Bessie 1918. His war service record shows he was Private 189103 621st AG.CO. Labour Corps.

Charles (Chas) Gliddon

Chas Gliddon was born at Sutcombe in 1885 and attended school in Bradworthy. He was the son of William, a farm labourer, born at Pancrasweek and Elizabeth who was also born at Sutcombe.

They lived at Broad Park, Bradworthy but by 1911 Chas had moved to Stroxworthy Farm where he was a horseman. They were a large family and his siblings were Carrie born in 1873, William in 1874, Albert born the following year, Mary Ellen in 1877, Thomas two years later, Norman 1880, Frederick 1883, Alice 1888, Reuben 1889 and finally Albert in 1900. Elizabeth, having given birth at least nine times, died in 1904 aged just 50. No further information is available on Chas.

Ernest Glover

Ernest Glover was born in Woolsery on 2nd February 1888 and attended school there from 1893 until 1901.He lived at Huddisford where his parents, Edward, who was born at Hartland according to the 1911 Census but at Woolsery in the 1901 version, farmed. His mother was Thirza a local girl. On leaving school Ernest became a cattleman on his father's farm. His brothers were William who was born in 1883 and at the age of 28 was a widower and self-employed tractor driver in 1911, and George

Record of Service

Army Form 2513.

~~ENROLMENT~~ PAPER

For men deemed to be enlisted in H.M. Regular Forces for General Service with the Colours or in the Reserve for the period of the War, under the provisions of the Military Service Act, 1916.

No. _____ Name *Ernest Glover* Corps **ROYAL REGIMENT OF ARTILLERY**

Questions to be put to the Reservist on ~~Enrolment.~~ *Joining*

1. What is your Name?	1. *Ernest Glover*
2. What is your full Address?	2. *Vern Cottage Woodbury Common*
3. Are you a British Subject?	3. *yes*
4. What is your Age?	4. *28* Years *11* Months
5. What is your Trade or Calling?	5. *Horseman*
6. Are you Married?	6. *yes*
7. Have you ever served in any branch of His Majesty's Forces, naval or military? If so, which?	7. *No*
8. Have you any preference for any particular branch of the service, if so, which?	8. *Garrison Artillery*
9. Are you desirous of serving in the Royal Navy, if so, state your qualifications.	9. *No*

I, *Ernest Glover* do solemnly declare that the above answers made by me to the above questions are true,

Ernest Glover SIGNATURE OF RECRUIT.

G Vincent Sergt Signature of Witness.

EXEMPTION FROM COMBATANT SERVICE ON CONSCIENTIOUS GROUNDS.

If the Recruit has been exempted by a Tribunal on conscientious grounds from serving as a combatant it should be so stated here_____

_____

MEDICAL CLASSIFICATION AS TO FITNESS FOR SERVICE ON ~~ENROLMENT.~~ *Joining*

Classification* _____

‡To be filled in by the Recruiting Officer after Classification by the Medical Board.

† Certificate of Approving Officer.

I approve the enrolment of the above-named man, and appoint him to the ‡ _____

Date _____ 19 . _____ Capt. R.F.A ‡ Approving Officer.

Place **HILSEA** _____

† The signature of the Approving Officer is to be affixed in the presence of the Recruit.
‡ Here insert the "Corps" to which the Recruit has been appointed.

who was born in 1892. He also had a sister Annie born in 1889. In the 1919 absent voters list Ernest was listed as having a next of kin at Venn Lane, this was the family home of his wife Blanche, née Johns, whom he married in the spring of 1914. He died 17th September 1963 aged 75.

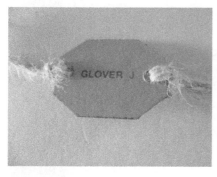

John Glover

John Glover was born in Parkham in 1872 and attended school there. His parents are believed to be Richard who was from Woolsery, and Parkham-born Elizabeth. They lived at Bitworthy Farm where his occupation was recorded as waggoner working for William Davey who was a farmer and mason. The other children of the marriage were Matilda born in 1874, James in 1880, William H, later known as Horace in 1883, Maud 1886 and Harriet 1885. He was the brother of Horace, who was farm foreman at Leyworthy 1930-1940. John was probably the oldest village member who served in this war, being over 40 when he signed up. Men of over 41 were being conscripted in the final months of the conflict.

William Glover

William was a farmer's son who took his horse to war. He was born on 25th June 1883 in Woolsery,

and died 2nd Nov 1951 living At Venn Hill, Woolsery. He attended Woolsery Primary School. His parents were Edward and Thirza Mary Glover née Eastabrook, and in 1911, William - a traction engine driver - was still living at home with parents in Huddisford. In 1912 William married Elison Brent in the district of Bideford. He had three siblings, Ernest, Annie and George. He did his War Service in the Devon Yeomanry. He was Loye Medd's grandfather.

Stanley Percival (Percy) Hatch

Percy Hatch was born on 2nd February 1900 at Clovelly but attended school at Woolsery between 1903 and 1914. He was the son of William, a rabbit trapper, who was born at Hatherleigh and Emma from Hartland. Rabbit trapping was a big business in the village at this time with several men being recorded as trappers or dealers. They lived in the village with their three children, the others being Mary born in 1881 and Albert 1894. Percy's war service records he was 70019 PTV 4th Res. Devons.

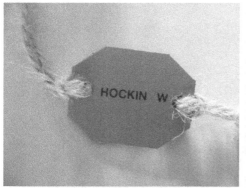

William Hockin

William was the son of Francis, who in turn was the son of Thomas and Ann who farmed 333 acres at Clifford, Woolsery. Francis and his wife Susan née Short had become farmers at Xeal or Zeal Farm, Petrockstowe, Dolton where they lived with their six children. Daughters Rose and Annie were dairymaids and like the third sister Bessie and their older brother, William who was born in 1883, all started their lives in Woolsery.

The family had reached Petrockstowe by the time Frank and John, the two youngest were born. It is believed locally that a man of this name was later a cobbler living at Green Cottage. A Devon regiment soldier recorded as W.J. Hocking was wounded in February 1916; this may or may not have been our man, probably not as I can find no reference to him having a second name.

Stanley Jenkin probably Jenkins

Stanley Jenkins was born in Buckland Brewer in 1890 and attended school there. He was the son of John and Emma, née Crocker, both born in Hartland and unusually both recorded as domestic servants/gardeners. Stanley and his elder siblings were all born in Buckland Brewer, but the family had by 1901 moved to Rollstone Cottage, Alwington, a five-roomed home, where they had fourteen children all of whom were alive in 1911.

The family also included William born 1889, Stanley 1890, Mark 1892, Frederick 1894, Florence 1896, John 1897, George 1899, Mary 1901, Percy 1904, Lilian 1905, Emmeline 1906, Ernest 1908 and Leslie the youngest born in 1910. There may have been more born; after the last census available Emma was at that time 43 years old. In 1911 Stanley was a servant working at the hotel in Woolsery. Although we have traced no descendants of Stanley it is fairly safe to suppose that he must have many relatives alive in the area today.

Thomas (Tom) Johns

Thomas Johns was born on 18th September 1893 at Clovelly but attended school in Woolsery. His parents were Walter, a farmer, and Rosa both Woolsery born, who had lived at Gorrell, and it appeared had recently moved to Seckington Farm, Higher Clovelly. Their other children were Albert born 1891, Wilfred 1895, William 1897, Emily 1899, Richard 1901 and Blanche 1903. Tom was described in one obituary as a young fellow of splendid physique.

Thomas worked on his father's farm before enlisting at Bideford. He served in the 11th Royal 1st

In Loving Memory of
Signaller Tom Johns
of Seckington Farm,
who was killed in action in Palestine
December 3rd, 1917.

Age 23 years.

Devon Yeomanry and Royal North Devon Hussars battery as 345911 Signaller. He had been in Palestine for about twelve months prior to his death. He was killed in action in Palestine on 3rd December 1917 just days before Jerusalem was liberated from the Turks, and he was buried in Jerusalem War Cemetery. A headstone in Woolsery churchyard commemorates his sacrifice: "Greater love have no man than this that he lay down his life for his friends." He was just 23 years old .

He was Uncle to Maurice, Raymond and Wilfred Heywood and Marianne Slee (née Heywood) and Great Uncle to Sally Jeffery (née Heywood), Tim and Keith Heywood, Joanne Walter (née Heywood), Rachel and Roger Heywood, and John Heywood.

The vicar F. Courtenay Burrough wrote "…that to him fell the honour of helping to deliver Palestine

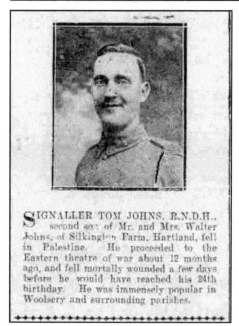

SIGNALLER TOM JOHNS, R.N.D.H., second son of Mr. and Mrs. Walter Johns, of Silkington Farm, Hartland, fell in Palestine. He proceeded to the Eastern theatre of war about 12 months ago, and fell mortally wounded a few days before he would have reached his 24th birthday. He was immensely popular in Woolsery and surrounding parishes.

out of the oppressive power of the Turks, and of aiding God's ancient people to return to the land from which they had been exiles for many hundreds of years. He was a dear fellow and beloved by all who knew him. He was a good son, and brother and a brave and cheerful soldier.

He never complained and his letters home were always bright and hopeful. To Mr. & Mrs. Walter Johns and family of Seckington, we offer our heartfelt sympathy in this time of their great sorrow. They are old friends, and were parishioners for many years. May God comfort them, and lead them to trust Him in the present darkness. We held a memorial service for him in our Church on Sunday Jan 13th and muffled peals were rung for him, he having been a ringer for many years."

His battalion signalling officer Lt. A.J.H. Dickinson wrote: "I knew Johns very well indeed as he had long time been a signaller in B Company and shortly before his death was attached to the battalion HQ signal section. His death was a real loss to the battalion for he was an excellent and reliable signaller and a thoroughly good fellow, in every way, always willing and cheerful, however hard the work and however trying the conditions.

I was not with the battalion on December 3rd but one of the other signallers who was with him at the time of his death, tells me they were caught by enfilade fire from a machine gun and Johns was killed instantly shot through the temple. This man Private Thomas, is positive his death was instant and painless."

Enfilade fire is where you engage the enemy formation from the flank. You generate enfilade fire, which strikes the enemy from the side.

Victor Moore

Victor Moore was born in Middlesex in 1893 and lived at Cranford Water Cottage with his grandparents Richard, a carpenter and wheelwright who had learned his trade with James Braund in the village, and Mary Moore. His sister Nellie, also born in Middlesex, lived there too. There appears to be no record of his parents, presumably one of Richard's three sons Noah, John or Richard was their father. Victor who was employed in 1911 as a teamster on a farm (actually wrongly transcribed as teamaker in one document) and ten years later as a lodger at the *Tradesman's Inn*, Bideford, but the latter document wrongly has him born in Woolfardisworthy, and his employment was recorded as a labourer.

George William Moore

George Moore was born in Black Torrington on 3rd January 1895. His parents were William Petherick Moore, a farmer, and Catherine Moore née Davey. The family, which included Elsie Kate born 1891, Stanley 1900 and Leonard 1903, moved to West Moor, Woolfardisworthy soon after George's birth and he attended school there, and Sunday school at Alminstone.

He is recorded as being a farmer's son working with horses in the census. In 1915 he married Ida May Boundy who was from Cranford, and the following year their daughter Dorothy was born. A second child, Ronald, was born in 1920. George was conscripted into the army where he served as Gunner 238661 R.F.A. and after training on Salisbury Plain set off for Italy where he was involved in conflict in the Asiago region according to post cards sent home to his wife.

On one such card, bearing a picture showing a church and houses, he recorded that he had passed these several times as there were near the front line, but the buildings were "now rather knocked about with shell fire". One incident he recalled in later years was the time when passing through a wine growing area he was given some wine, which he rather enjoyed. Later he saw people treading the grapes with their feet and he didn't fancy it again. He sent a Special Forces festive card in 1918 saying "A Merry Christmas from Italy". It appears he returned home to West Moor in 1919.

In March 1920 George and Ida's son Ronald was born and a few weeks later they took over the tenancy of a small farm at Hiscott near Barnstaple. In 1927 they bought Luppincott Farm, Alverdiscott which was a larger concern a few miles away. An unexpected surprise occurred in September 1934; their second son Kenneth arrived and it is to him we are indebted for much of this information.

In October 1944 Ron married Mary Lee and took over Luppincott. George and Ida then moved to Lovacott Green Farm, Newton Tracey where they remained until son Ken married Muriel Wright in 1961. Their final move was to Bishops Tawton where George

This is where I used to go for
rations when I was doing drivers
work. It is right on top of the
mountain. The train climbs the
side of the mountain on cogs.
The cogs are laid in between the
rails & there is a cog wheel under
the engine that works on them.

I have been through this place
several times. It is near the front
line. But it does not look exactly
like this now. The houses & church
are knocked rather out of shape
with shell fire. I have had to put
on rather a jildy move a time or
two going through it when he has
been shelling it.

Loos The Somme Ecoust-Croissilles
Givenchy The Ancre Bullecourt
Festubert Broodseinde Ridge
Neuve
Chapelle Beutel
Ypres Asiago Plateau Italy

A merry Christmas
to you all
From Italy

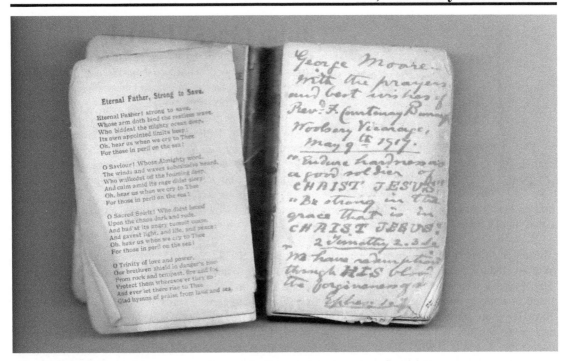

was living when he died in 1976. The family have postcards he sent from the front, a copy of the New Testament which they believe Vicar Courtney Burrough presented to him when he was conscripted, and his war medals.

Members of the Moore family still live and farm at West Moor.

Richard Moore

Richard Moore was born on 7th June 1865 in Woolsery and attended the village school. His parents were Richard, a self employed carpenter, and Eliza Jane who lived at Cross Park. His paternal grandfather was also called Richard.

Eliza Jane died in the early years of the twentieth century and her widower then married Emily and they lived at West Bucks. There are no other children recorded from the first marriage or the second. Richard Moore, the youngest, was also a carpenter and in 1911 was a boarder at William Crocker's hotel in the village. Among the residents was Bessie, daughter of the hotelier, and in 1913 she married Richard. He saw war service as Wheeler 145941 in A Battery of the Royal Horse Artillery. As a wheeler, he was a private in the gunnery divisions probably working at getting the guns prepared and into position, as well as maintaining them His gravestone records that he returned from the war and lived a long life, dying in 1949 aged 89. His son, a fourth Richard, died in May 1955 aged 69.

John (Jack) Peard

Jack Peard was born on the 13th October 1890 at Horns Cross. He attended school first at Holwell, the former school building on the main road near *Hoops Inn*, then transferred to Woolsery.

Holwell School had begun life in 1876 as an infant school set up by Parkham's school board, but like some other similarly designated ones it allowed children to stay on up to Standard IV. It closed its doors as a school in 1921 and is now somewhat extended and is a private house. Jack's parents were William, a farm labourer, and Elizabeth. The family had lived at Horns Cross hamlet before moving to Woolsery village.

The other children of their marriage were Mary born in 1874, Ann 1875, Sarah 1876, Giles 1878, William 1882, Edward 1884, Charles 1886 and Alice 1889. Giles is believed to have been the father of Tom Peard, a well known village character until his death in the early eighties. Jack's occupation was listed as working on roads, and died in 1970 aged 79. His war service was with A.BR 4620 63rd Royal Navy Division, but he was discharged after a few months training as he was deemed medically unfit, and never actually served. The 63rd (Royal Naval) Division was an infantry division which served during the First World War. It was originally formed as the Royal Naval Division at the outbreak of the war, from Royal Navy and Royal Marine reservists and volunteers who were not needed for service at sea.

He is believed to have lived at Venn, now the Bannister's house, before it was enlarged.

William & Dorothy Pennington

William John Pennington

William John Pennington was born on the 18th of July 1894, the son of John & Sarah Jane (née Westlake) at Bradninch, near Cullompton, Devon. Their other children included Mary Grace born in 1878 and died in 1882, Sarah 1880, Rosina was born within twelve months, Arthur Thomas born in 1888, Ethel in 1892, Frederick 1898 and Charles Frank born two years later.

According to the 1911 Census they had had ten children, of which seven survived and three sons still lived at home whilst William was lodging with the Bolton family in Kilmington, Axminster as an apprentice carpenter, and Rosina was a domestic servant in Seaton. During the Great War, William served with both the Devon Regiment and the Duke of Cornwall's Light Infantry (DCLI) but not until conscription was introduced.

In an article in the *Western Morning News* entitled "Bideford Rural Tribunals" dated 9th March 1916, it was claimed that he was needed to help on the farm as a cattleman. This was refuted along with many others, and sometime in 1916 William

Sarah, Arthur & William Pennington (Cranford)

Pennington was enlisted as 21700 Pte Pennington into the 12th (Labour) Battalion, Devon Regiment.

This Regiment was formed in Devonport in May 1916 and landed in France to join the Fourth Army in the following month. The labour battalions were allotted to the Devonshire Regiment with whom they had only the most tenuous connection - one or two invalided Devon officers served with them. Men in these Battalions undertook arduous, occasionally dangerous, support jobs behind the lines. Within months the connection with the Devonshire Regiment was disbanded, and the battalion was transferred to the newly formed Labour Corps in April 1917, as 152nd and 153rd labour companies.

It is presumed at this point Private Pennington was transferred to the 2nd Battalion Devons, as can be seen in his entry onto the DCLI medal roll, rather than to the Labour Corps. The 2nd Devons were involved in lots of fighting from 1917, and although the family think that Pte Pennington was involved in Passchendale, Ypres, Somme and Vimy Ridge this cannot be proven. There is photographic evidence of Pte Pennington wearing two wound stripes, these were issued to men injured during the war, and were worn on the sleeve of the left

forearm. There is also a newspaper clipping from the *Western Times*, dated Friday 31 August 1917, stating that Pte W. J Pennington of Woolsery had been injured. It is also thought within the family that Pte Pennington was possibly injured a third time, although this cannot be proven either.

It is known within the family that William Pennington was sent back to the military hospital in Stonehouse, Plymouth at least twice, meeting his future wife, Dorothy Blanche (née Hayman) of Plympton St Maurice there. The 2nd Devons had taken a mauling in early 1918, and were sent to a quiet sector to recuperate. However, the area was chosen by the Germans to launch a large offensive. They were being held in reserve, but were pushed up to the front to hold the line.

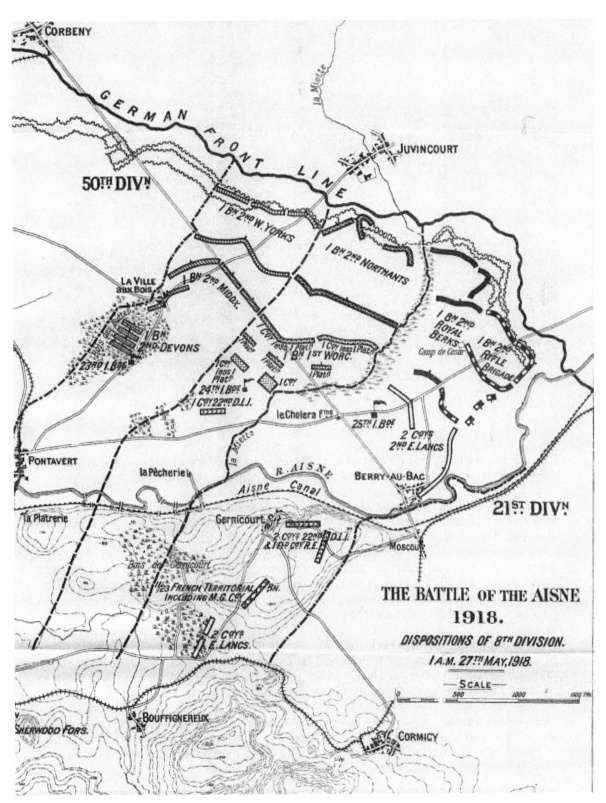

Dispositions of the 8th Division at 0100 hours on 27 May 1918, showing the location of the
2nd Devons on Bois des Buttes.

The Last Stand of the 2nd Devons by William Barnes Wollen.

They did this at a heavy cost; 24 officers and 528 men either killed, wounded or missing. This became a famous action known as "Bois De Buttes".

As William was neither a casualty nor a survivor of this action it is thought that he had been wounded in the heavy fighting prior to the Battalion being sent to the quiet sector to recuperate. Thus he missed Bois Des Buttes and so we can consider his wound a lucky one! *The Hartland and West Country Chronicle* reported on 21st September 1917 that Private W.J. Pennington had officially been reported wounded. William Pennington was sent to the 10th Battalion DCLI and his service number changed to 30196, presumably this was because the 2nd Devons had been wiped out. In all known photographs of William in uniform, he is always wearing a Devon Regiment cap badge, which would indicate that he only spent the end of the war in the DCLI.

After the war, William used to cycle from Woolsery to Plympton to see Dorothy; this was a round trip of over 120 miles. In 1921 they married and set up home at Bucks Cross where William worked at Walland Cary as a carpenter and handy man. In 1940 they moved across the road to Bucks Cross Stores which Dorothy ran until 1952, when they moved to Little Stowford, Bradworthy.

Twelve years later they moved again, this time to Okehampton. On 4th January 1969, Dorothy passed away. 18 months later on 12th June 1970, William also passed away, whilst staying with his daughter in Bristol. Both were interred at Okehampton. The children of William and Dorothy were Kenneth John, Herbert William, Frederick George, Ivor Stuart , Frank, and Bernice Jane.

Private Pennington was the grandfather of Stuart , Jill, Linda and Nigel Pennington among others and his great grandchildren included Nick Piper to whom we are grateful for this research and collation of his forefather's war service.

[The Perkins or occasionally Perkin family below were recorded with and without the "s" on different national documents.]

James Perkins

James Perkins was born on January 25th 1898 in Woolsery and attended the village school. He was the son of James and Elizabeth Perkins who farmed at Venn. He was one of a large family which included John born in 1882, Emily 1883, Vida 1884, Jesse 1885, Richard 1889, William 1890, Thomas 1891, Elizabeth 1892, Albert 1894, Olive 1895, Frederick 1898 and Walter 1901.

James worked on the family farm and was later a slaughter man living at Green Cottage and farmed the fields where Manor Park is now situated. Three of his brothers also served in the war. He was Gunner 238662 in the Royal Field Artillery. He died on 19th May 1949 aged 51 years.

John Perkins

John Perkins was born on the 27th July 1882 at Woolsery and attended the village school. He was the eldest child of James and Elizabeth Perkins who farmed at Venn. His siblings were Emily born 1883, Vida 1884, Jesse 1885, Richard 1889, William 1890, Thomas 1891 Elizabeth 1892 Albert 1894, Olive 1895, James 1896, Frederick 1898 and Walter 1901. Having such a large family James Perkins was determined that as soon as they were old enough they were all sent out to work.

John was employed as a teamster at Lane Barton. He emigrated to Canada in 1916 and joined the Canadian expeditionary forces and returned to serve in the U.K, Belgium and France, eventually returning to the village in 1919.

It is believed he decided that to join the expeditionary force was the easiest way to return to his native land; fortunately he survived the fields of battle. It appears that many men who had emigrated to Commonwealth countries and couldn't afford to return to their roots took this rather extreme method of getting home, some no doubt to bring their lives to a premature end. His three brothers also went to war.

William (also Willie or Bill) Perkins

William Perkins was born 13th September 1890 at Woolsery and attended school there. His parents, as with the two previous heroes, were James and Elizabeth who farmed at Venn. He later lived in the village and is described as a general labourer. His siblings were John born 1882, Emily 1883, Vida 1884, Jesse 1885, Richard 1889, Thomas 1891 Elizabeth 1892 Albert 1894, Olive 1895, James 1896, Frederick 1898 and Walter 1901. He married Amelia Nina May Lee in 1911, and their children were Kathryn, Bill, Elsie and Walter.

William died 29th June 1974 aged 83 years and Nina, as she was known, on 19th November 1972 aged 94. Local connections include his grandson Peter Wood and his great granddaughter Carol Wood of Langtree.

Albert Perkins

Albert Perkins was born on 19th August 1895 at Woolsery, where he attended school and died 16th May 1967 aged 71 years.

His parents were also James, a farmer and Elizabeth living at Venn His siblings were John 1882, Emily 1883, Vida 1884, Jesse 1885, Richard 1889, William 1890, Thomas 1891 Elizabeth 1892, Olive 1895, James 1896, Frederick 1898 and Walter 1901.

His occupation is described as a horseman on his father's farm.

He married Annie Jennings and lived at Cross Park. They had four children Dorothy, Beatrice Amy, Jessie and Albert Cecil who became a carpenter. He died May 1967 aged 71.

As above his three brothers also went to war. He signed up as private 204256 and later he was a private in W.C.L.C.L.C. number 640451 according to the absent voters list.

Some of his descendants live at Buckland Brewer.

George Pickard

George was born in Bideford 1886 to John, an insurance agent, and Laura Pickard. They lived at Albert Place, Old Town, Bideford in 1901 and he later resided at Fairholme, Woolsery. Their other children were Laura born 1877, Agnes 1879, Emma 1882, Mary 1884, Alice 1888 and Walter 1893.

George's occupation was described as an apprentice shoe maker in 1901, but later he was said to have been a road foreman for the council. He possibly married Maud Cann, a domestic servant at Littleham, in 1912. He was a cousin of C.J. Andrew.

Lionel Prance

In 1888 Lionel Prance was born at Bradworthy, where he attended school. His family lived at Muddy Corner. His parents were William, a labourer, and Elizabeth and they had three other children; William born 1896, Mary in 1900 and James two years later. They moved to Alminstone Cottage, Woolsery. After the war he married Dorothy M. Burt at Launceston, and then disappears from the record system.

Francis (Frank) Cory Prouse

Frank Prouse was born on the 3rd December 1889 and attended Woolsery School. His parents were John Cory Prouse, a carpenter and former hotelkeeper, and Mary née Shute, and they lived in the village

The family consisted of Alice born in 1878, Jane in 1880, William 1884, Lily 1886, Florence 1887, Frank 1889, Harry 1891, 1894, and the youngest was John Thomas 1894. Lily sadly died aged 11 in 1897 as did two other unnamed siblings. Frank, like his father, became a carpenter and married Elsie Maud Johns in 1925. Frank's father John owned a few acres of land about a quarter of a mile from the village centre along the road to Clovelly, where - as a master carpenter - he had a workshop. Frank, having become a carpenter too, built his own workshop there, and then his own house known - then and now - as "The Laurels." His father assisted him in this project.

Frank signed up at Bideford in July 1917 for the Royal

Marine Light Infantry and was sent to Plymouth for training. Six months later he was a member of the British Expeditionary Forces fighting the enemy in Northern France. Whilst there he sent home some unusual postcards to his fiancée. They had no message and the complete front face had a floral design of coloured silk threads. Some of these were displayed in a picture frame on the wall of the house during the Second World War when Roy and John Brushett were billeted with them as evacuees.

In early March 1918, engaging the enemy at Havrincourt Wood - which was about ten miles from Cambrai - a shell exploded very close to him, killing all of his nearby comrades. He suffered shot and shrapnel wounds to his body and left leg. Subsequently an army surgeon cut off the leg with a red hot saw to prevent gangrene setting in.

The vicar, in his magazine of April in that year, shared the sad news that Frank Prouse had been severely injured in France. He stated that "at first the worst was feared and great sympathy was manifested for his father, sisters and brothers. (Mary, his mother, had died early in 1916, aged 63.) But we have much to thank God for, in that although one leg was amputated his life has been spared and his wounds are healing. He has written most bravely and cheerfully and we much admire his courage and are thankful his life has been spared for us by a miracle. Surely God has heard our prayers for our men because of 54 who joined up so few have been killed."

Frank returned from battle on a stretcher to Plymouth Hospital where treatment and convalescence helped his physical and mental recovery. During the following year he was fitted with a full length aluminium leg, rehabilitated and enabled to return to Woolsery on 5th April 1919. He became one of the village's better known war heroes after he returned with his artificial limb. One of his favourite expressions was "Kick my leg...... it will hurt you more than it hurts me."

On returning from war duties Frank married his fiancée Elsie Maud Johns, daughter of William and Fanny, née Burnard from Cornwall, Johns, who farmed at Dyke Green Farm Higher Clovelly. He took on an apprentice, Cecil Perkins of Woolsery to learn carpentry and help finish off The Laurels which was finally completed in 1920. His father John died on March 18th 1937, aged 88.

His craftsmanship with wood enabled him to make a very wide range of farm equipment, gates of all shapes and sizes, domestic furniture and coffins. At Christmas time he used oddments of wood to make toys, dolls house furniture and so on. Roy mentions that of special interest to him was a model farmyard wheelbarrow built to scale for a boy of eleven. His skills were of the highest order and some said he was a perfectionist.

He was the uncle of Beryl Hancock and Alan, and Royston Johns. His wife was their father's sister. Beryl reports that one of her lasting memories was watching him rub methylated spirits into the stump of his leg, supposedly to harden it and ease the pain and discomfort, and that she and her brothers spent many happy hours at The Laurels with Uncle Frank. Another youngster with a long memory of Frank's missing leg was Roy Brushett who still remembers his first night in Woolsery as an evacuee. "[Mrs Prouse] held a small lamp as we went upstairs and entered a large bedroom. There we were introduced to Uncle Frank who was sitting up in a large double bed. After a few words I was asked which of the two beds we would like to sleep in. The other bed was a small double. For some unexplainable reason I chose the one Uncle Frank was in. As he moved to get out, I noticed that he only had one leg, whereupon I immediately changed my mind and went to the other bed".

Elsie died on 22nd April 1948 aged 55 and Frank on April 17th 1968 aged 78 years. Three of his brothers and a brother-in-law also went to war. Grateful thanks to Beryl and Roy for supplying information about this remarkable war hero whom they both clearly held in very high regard.

Harry (Plummy) Prouse

Harry was born on 14th May 1891 and attended Woolsery School. He was the son of John, a carpenter and former hotelkeeper, and Mary, and they lived in the village.

He did not become a carpenter like his father and elder brother, but a farm labourer and later a quarry man opposite Strouds breaking stones. He had ground and a shed at Irene and milked his cows there before and after work.

His war service saw him working as a horseman.

Harry's three brothers and brother-in-law also went to war. He was nicknamed Plummy and died aged just 41 with heart problems on June 11th 1932. He was married to Clara Elizabeth, and was father of Dorothy who later married F.T. Knight. He was the grandfather of Lorna Harding.

(John) Thomas Prouse

Thomas Prouse was born on the 18th September 1893 and attended Woolsery School. He was the son of John, a carpenter and former hotelkeeper, and his wife Mary; they lived in a four-roomed house in the village. The family consisted of Alice born in 1878, Jane in 1880, William 1884, Lily 1886, Florence 1887, Frank 1889, Harry 1891, 1894, and the youngest was John Thomas 1894. Lily sadly died aged 11 in 1897 as did two other unnamed siblings.

Thomas became a carpenter no doubt joining the family firm. He married Mabel Trace in 1924. Like his brothers he joined the army and rose to become T2/016200SGT. A sergeant in the 56th div. Army Service Corps. This was a unit of over 300,000 men who kept the front lines supplied with food, ammunition and equipment.

William (Bill) Prouse

Bill Prouse was born on September 3rd 1883 in the village and attended Woolsery School. His parents were John, a carpenter and former hotelkeeper, and Mary.

The family consisted of Alice born in 1878, Jane in 1880, William 1884, Lily 1886, Florence 1887, Frank 1889, Harry 1891, 1894, and the youngest was John Thomas 1894. Lily sadly died aged 11 in 1897 as did two other unnamed siblings In 1901 Bill's occupation was coal carrier in 1901, but in 1911 he had become a mail driver. He married Emma and had a daughter

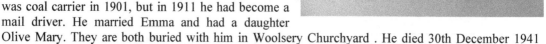

Olive Mary. They are both buried with him in Woolsery Churchyard . He died 30th December 1941 aged 58. There is no record to date of his service history.

Fortunately all four brothers returned from the war!

Thomas Curtis Rowe

Thomas was born in Hartland in 1890 to Lewis and Emma Rowe

Their home was at one time at Elmscott, Hartland, but he lived in Bideford at the time of his signing up.

He enlisted at Bideford as a private at Gallipoli with the Household cavalry & cavalry of the line which included the Royal North Devon Hussars and yeomanry. He was admitted to St. George's Hospital Malta 16/12/15 with severe frostbite, he was presumed to have been well enough to return to England, but died of enteric fever (typhoid) on 29th May the following year. His death is recorded on the Woolsery and Bideford memorials but no direct link to the village can be found.

In Memory of

Private

Thomas Curtis Rowe

800, 3rd/1st Bn., Royal North Devon Hussars who died on 28 May 1916 Age 26

Son of the late Lewis and Emma Rowe, of Hartland, Devon.

Remembered with Honour
Hursley (All Saints) Church Cemetery

Commemorated in perpetuity by
the Commonwealth War Graves Commission

R.N.D.H. AT GALLIPOLI.

Barum Sergeant's Interesting Account of the Landing.

IN A "GROUSE-BOX": RISKY WORK

Samuel Searle

There appears to be no-one of this name that can be found who was associated with the village, and yet his name is there quite clearly on the memorial. There are three possible people of that name.

One was one born at South Molton in 1880, he was the son of another Samuel and born at Holsworthy, who is probably the most likely one. The outsider is one born at Axminster unlikely but interesting because in the 1911 Census is one of three members of his family who are recorded as toilet brush makers, including his eldest sister who is a toilet brush polisher! A Samuel Searle died at Stratton aged just 29 in 1928.

Frederick William (Fred) Shaddick

Fred Shaddick was born in Bradworthy in 1892 and probably attended school there. He was the son of William a labourer and Mary who also had two daughters Emily born 1889 and Annie who was five years older than her sister.

In 1901 the family lived at Trentworthy Cottage, Bradworthy. He was a general farm worker before and after the war for Albert Cann at Hurley Meadow, where he was living in 1911. He later lived at Claw Cross and for the last fourteen years of his life at East Park. He died on 20th October 1982 aged 90.

May. 1963.

'UNCLE FRED LOOKS BACK

Fifty-three years on same farm

A BRADWORTHY farm worke who has known four generation of the same family and has bee "Uncle Fred" to three of then completes 53 years work this year a Hurley Meadow, Woolsery.

He is 71-year-old Mr. Fred Shaddick, of Claw Cross.

"I came here when I was 19, back in 1910," recalled Mr. Shaddick, "and I'm still here. When you're content, what's the sense in changing?"

Although he suffers with arthritis, Mr. Shaddick still finds plenty to keep him busy.

"There was a time when I could walk after horses ploughing from daylight to dark in the spring and think nothing of it," he mused.

But even the ice and snow and bitter cold of last winter could not keep him home. His present employer, Mr. Dennis Stevens—the grandson of Mr. Albert Cann, who first took him on at Hurley Meadow

MR. FRED SHADDICK

—drove the tractor down to fetch Mr. Shaddick every morning. And although the farmyard was a sheet of ice, Mr. Shaddick only fell once.

Mechanisation is the biggest change he has seen in farming. "There are altogether different ways of farming today from what it used to be," he said.

"We used to cut the corn with a reaper and follow behind binding the corn into sheaves under our arm as we went.

"The cornfield was a place of fun in those days. Four or five binders, somebody driving the horse, another man sending the sheaves, and a prong for it best up at the head of the field.

Edwin Stacey

There is an Edwin Stacey named on the Woolsery Church memorial, but we have had difficulty locating him. Edwin Stacey, Private 30841 Devon Regiment born Nether Stowey, Somerset died of injuries on the Somme 28th July 1917 but 'ours' clearly survived and I can find no Devon connection with this man.

The nearest Stacey family was at Stafford Moor, Langtree but again none with a similar Christian name. There was an Edwin Thomas Stacey, a butcher born to a Londoner in Hatherleigh, but again there are no obvious links.

Richard Stevens

Richard was born on 13th February 1878 to Robert and Emily Stevens who lived at Stevens Cottage, Huddisford Moor. There were five other children of the marriage; John born in 1878, Sarah born the following year and Archibald 1883, Ada was born in 1884 and Regina a year later. Richard was recorded as a farm servant at Marshall Farm in 1901, and as a waggoner at Rectory Farm, Morwenstow in 1911.

It is believed that he lived at Cranford and Sessacott, Putford after the war. His war service was T/422769DVR 662nd Co.Army Service Corps. He died 5th October 1949 aged 71.

Archibald (Archie) Stevens

Archie was born on 27th February 1883 to Robert, a farm labourer, and Emily Stevens who lived at Stevens Cottage, Huddisford Moor. He attended Woolsery School. There were five other children of the marriage: John born in 1878, Sarah born the following year and Richard, his fellow soldier in 1882, Ada born 1884 and Regina 1885. In 1901 his employment was described as in charge of cattle at Gorvin, Hartland but by 1911 he was a general farm worker at Lane Barton. He enlisted at Bideford and was Private 202285 in the 7th Battalion Worcester regiment.

On November 17th he returned home to marry Miriam Cawsey of Northam. He returned to France on the 21st having taken his wife to visit the vicar at Cranford on the 19th from their home at Northam. He was killed on the 29th November 1917 aged 34, officially in France and Flanders which means, in reality, the Somme.

The vicar recorded that "He looked so happy when we saw him. How little we thought how near he was to the end of his life! But he was a godly young fellow, quiet and consistent, so we know

that his as a 'home call'. I think all who knew him felt a love for him, and join in the sorrow of his parents and brothers and sisters. He gave his life for us, and we honour his memory, and give our sincere sympathy to his distressed widow and relatives." A memorial service was to be held later. He is remembered with honour at Fauberg D'Amines Cemetery Arras, Pas de Calais where 2,647 casualties of war are buried.

(Richard) Percy Thomas

Percy Thomas was born in Bradworthy on June 28th 1890, he attended school there, then his family moved to Woolsery so he transferred to the village school. His father was called Richard and was a "groom and gardener, not domestic", and his mother was Harriet, who was born in Liverpool.

His homes included Walkhampton on Dartmoor, then Bradworthy, and then the village. The family later moved on to Swimbridge, but Percy stayed on working as a rabbit trapper and living with Samuel Vanstone.

His family included three sisters and a brother. Ada born in 1888, Herbert 1892, Joan 1896 and Kate 1899. He married Maria Brent daughter of Reuben a wheelwright and carpenter in Woolsery in 1912. They had three children Herbert, Peter and Joan. Percy lived in Swimbridge in later life and when Woolsery School celebrated its centenary in 1979 he was the oldest former pupil, aged 89, who was fit enough to attend, and as guest of honour he cut the cake.

He was Gunner 116979 in the 275th Siege Battery Royal Gunnery Artillery and almost certainly saw action at Ypres. He died a widower late in 1983 aged 93, Maria having previously expired aged 83 in 1972.

Albert Edward Trathen

Albert was born in 1885 in Kensington, London.

His parents were Jamin, a farmer who had earlier lived at Little Duerdon Farm, Woolsery before moving to London, although I am unable to discover what precisely he was doing there. His three children were all born in Kensington. Jamin married in 1881 but I have been unable to discover the name of his wife who does not appear to have been on the scene when he returned from London to farm at Moorhead, sometime before 1901; this may have been Little Duerdon renamed. He had two daughters Jane Florence born 1883 and Elsie Maud 1887, both of whom came with him

Albert married Effie Truscott Hicks, the school master's daughter, in 1909. Her parents had left Devon five years earlier and her father was now an assistant master in Islington and a widower. Albert and Effie had three children, Effie Jane who was born to them in 2010, Isobel a year later and Albert in 1913. He was by now the farmer himself at Moor Head but when the two younger children commenced their education he was recorded as living in the village. He was the grandfather of Charles and Mary Wade.

He saw war service as 520223 Private 654th AG.CO.L.C.

William John Tyrell

William was another Londoner born in Hackney in 1885. His parents were Arthur, a cellar man, in a wine cellar and Fanny, and he had a brother, also called Arthur. They were all still in London.

In 1911 he was working as a farm labourer and living in Back Street, in the village, with John Cory Prouse and Lilian Prouse his in-laws, Jane his wife, whom he had married in 1909, their son William John who had not yet had his first birthday and his two brothers in law.

The house contained four rooms including the kitchen! A second child, Lily, was born the following year.

His daughter Lily was twice kept at home for a period of time and then re-admitted to Woolsery School. This may have been due to sickness as schools were inclined to take children off the role for longer bouts of sickness to enhance their attendance percentages. However Lily lived until she was 75 so could not have been too sickly. No record of his war service has been discovered, but he removed to Weare Giffard with his family in 1919.

Thomas Frederick Wade

Thomas was the only son of Frederick, a carpenter, and Elizabeth Wade. He was born on 23rd April 1899 at Ashmansworthy and attended Woolsery School. He had a sister Charlotte born in 1894 and his grandmother, also Charlotte Wade, a widow lived with the family.

Thomas was still at school when the census of 1911 was completed not having reached his twelfth birthday. 103 years later his daughter Mary still lived in the house while Charlie, his son, resided at Bradworthy. He left home to become Aircraftsman 98255 A/M2 A.R.S. 2nd class

Mark Westaway

Mark Westaway was born 24th January 1897 in Woolsery and attended the village school. His parents Thomas, a farmer and carriage builder, and Asenath lived in the village. In 1911 they had an eight-roomed house, and as well as their daughter and three sons they had two servants, both from Putford, living in their home. One was described as a general farm worker and the other as a "wagoner on the farm" both working for Thomas Westaway.

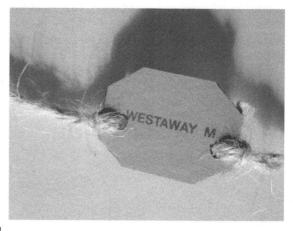

The children of the household were Catherine aged 20 and described as a dairy worker at home, Stanley, two years younger, and working on the farm, Mark 12, and Wilfred 11, both still at school.

Mark later lived at West Villa and is a relative of Cyril (Alwington) and Mark Westaway.

James Wonnacott

James Wonnacott was born in 1883 in Clovelly and attended school there. His parents: John, a labourer, and Mary had two sons, the other being William born 1894, and a daughter Gertrude born in 1891   The family lived at Stoop Dyke Cottage, Clovelly in 1901.

By 1911 James had moved to Little Highworthy, and like his father he was a farm labourer. He had married Charlotte in 1908 and had two children Charles aged two and John born a year later. Subsequently they had five more children: George born later that year,

Wilfred in 1911, Leslie 1914, Olive born in 1917 and Alfred three years later. James married Charlotte in 1908 and they had seven children over the next twelve years, the others were Charles born the following year, John 1910, George 1911, Wilfred 1913, Leslie 1914 , Olive 1917 and finally Alfred in 1920.

James is believed to have been a chimney sweep and horse breaker, in his post war life, living in Chapel Street, Woolsery. Bill Souch and Martin Wonnacott were his grandsons, the latter was at one time landlord at the *Coach and Horses Inn*. There is no record of his war service, however Woolsery's one fatal casualty in the 1939 war was Harold Wonnacott, who could have been his grandson.

The following group of men do not appear on the Woolsery war memorial but do appear on the absent voters list of 1919, and therefore quite clearly have Woolsery connections.

Leonard Johns

Leonard Johns was born on 29th February 1897 according to the School records, a date which never existed but he was certainly born in the first quarter of 1897. He started school at Clovelly and then transferred to Woolsery in 1904 and attended there for six years.

He was part of a large family, Charles born 1894, Edward in 1896, Leonard, Charlotte 1899 and Ida 1900, Mary 1901, Richard 1903, Lily 1905, and Frederick 1908. It is recorded that Richard and Mary had ten children prior to the 1911 Census and nine were still living. They were all born in Woolsery.

Their home was at Clifford Cottage in 1901 and 1911, it had four rooms. Ten years earlier Richard had been a farm labourer at West Town Farm. At the age of 13 Leonard was recorded as a cow boy (not cowboy) at the same farm, which was owned by Miss Mary Cruse. Later Tom went to live and work at West Dyke farm and it was from there that he lied about his age in order to join Kitchener's army.

A cutting from the *Bideford Gazette* dated November 18th 1915 records that among those enlisting were Leonard Johns and William Babb both from Clovelly and both joining the Devons. He had enrolled in the Devon Regiment (20765) and was wounded in the leg soon after his arrival in France, but six weeks later had recovered sufficiently to return to the trenches. He later transferred to the Machine Gun Corps (13480) presumably soon after it was founded in October 1916. He was killed on the Somme on the sixteenth of October 1916, aged just 19, when a shell killed him and two of his comrades. The following is an extract from the Gazette.

Pte. Leonard Johns, of Clovelly, left West Dyke Farm, where he had been living for four years, and put on his age in order to join Kitchener's Army. He was wounded in his legs by shrapnel soon after his arrival in France, but in six weeks had recovered sufficiently to return to the trenches. Then a shell killed him and two comrades. In writing to his parents his officer said: "As his officer I cannot express how much I shall miss him from my section. He was always cheerful in the most adverse circumstances, and was willing to obey my and my sergeant's orders at all times, and was liked by all of us. You have a great consolation in that he did his duty to the end and was a brave soldier." On Sunday, at Providence Chapel, a memorial service was conducted.

A letter to his parents stated, "As his officer I cannot express how much I shall miss him from my section. He was always cheerful in the most adverse circumstances and was willing to obey my and my sergeant's orders at all times, and was liked by all of us. You have a great consolation in that he did his duty to the end and was a brave soldier." On Sunday at Providence Chapel a memorial service was conducted and muffled bells were rung.

Just twelve days earlier his friend William Babb, who had signed up with him, had also been killed in the same area. He was the son of William and May Ann of Burscott Cotttage, Clovelly. His officer also wrote of him that he was an extremely brave man always ready to face danger.

It is with thanks to David Regan of Glasgow that our attention has been drawn to Leonard Johns, a Woolsery man, who at the time of joining lived near Clovelly. He died in the war and is not named on either the Woolsery or Clovelly Memorials.

Albert Collings

Albert was born in Cornwall. In the 1901 and 1911 Census he recorded Stratton as his birth place but in 1881 his parents John, a farm labourer, and his wife Elizabeth indicated that all their family were born at their current home in Trebarwith, a tiny village near Tintagel. He was certainly Cornish as were his sisters Elizabeth and Mary, Albert being the youngest.

At some stage in his life Albert crossed the border to live and work, and the 1901 Census finds him listed as a navvy living at the home of his father-in-law John Ashton, a road contractor and employer

whom presumably was his boss as they worked for Bideford Rural District Council.

Also in the house were John's wife, Mary - a Woolsery girl - four daughters and a son, and also Hilda the four week old daughter of Albert.

He had married Eva Ashton the previous year but she does not seem to be mentioned in the census there or anywhere else. Both she and her daughter are mentioned in the following year as they both died in the Autumn of 1902.

Just over a year later Albert married again, this time Rosina Snow was his bride. She was the daughter of John and Jane Snow of Hartland.

The couple went on to have six children: Frederick John, Minnie, Arthur John, William Henry, Albert who died aged two, and Thomas who died in 1918 aged just six.

It is perhaps unsurprising that two of his sons were given the second name of John as his own father and both father-in-laws bore that name. Albert had attested to the Army reserve on 11th December 1915, continuing to work on the local roads, but was not mobilised as a private until the first day of February in 1918. Being a road man he was posted as a Pioneer to the Road Construction Company, Royal Engineers Regiment number 40640. Four months later he was off to Dar-Es Salaam in East Africa and gained promotion to Sapper in October 1918, and some six weeks later was raised to corporal, still at Dar-Es-Salaam. By now the war was over but presumably there was still much road building to do. He was demobilised in May the following year.

He returned home to once again work on the roads and died in 1936 aged 55, his address is recorded as Fonchole Woolsery [sic]. He also lived at West Bucks and was the grandfather of Albert, who has confirmed him to be the third man from the right in the vicar's row in the group photo, and Margaret. It is strange that Albert does not make the war memorial listing and yet was in the photo line up. He was awarded the Victory Medal and British War Medal.

Samuel Thomas Sleep Cowling

Thomas was born late in 1893 at Davidstow in Cornwall and was baptised on 11th February the following year at Treglasta Bridge, Davidstow. He was the son of Susanna Rowe Cowling, a single mother, and had at least one sibling sister, Margaret Alberta. There was a married farm labourer living nearby called Samuel Sleep. Is this a clue as to his other parent?

Samuel joined the Royal Navy as boy entrant J6583 in January 1910 and then signed on for twelve years on the 3rd December 1911. He at some stage found himself in Huddersfield, where he met and

married Sarah A. Whiteley in 1921 and they had a son John a year later. As a boy sailor he served on HMS *Impregnable*, HMS *Leviathan* and then as an ordinary seaman on HMS *Vanguard*, HMS *King Alfred*, HMS *Endeavour* and HMS *Dublin* between December 1911 until May 1914.

He then became an Able Seaman serving on HMS *Dublin*, HMS *Vivid II (Opposum)*, HMS *Diligence*, HMS *Vanessa II*, HMS *Blake* and HMS *Valiant* until June 1920. He then became a Leading Seaman on HMS *Valiant* before moving to HMS *King George V* and HMS *Columbine* where he ended his service in December 1923.

It is believed he lived at Venn Farm at some time, presumably between demobilisation and his death on 3rd December 1971 at Upper Agbrigg, Yorkshire. Having such a distinctive name it is difficult to confuse him with anyone else, but having married a Yorkshire girl he chose to spend his later life in the north.

Wilfred Thomas Davey

Wilfred was born 14th November 1891 at Woolsery, where he attended the village school. His parents were Robert and Elizabeth Emily Davey who were living at Bucks Mills with her father, Simon Crews, a miller. Robert was a mason and Wilfred had followed his father into that trade by 1911 when the three of them lived in a seven-roomed house at Bucks Cross. His only sibling was Studley Crews Davey who was born in 1895 and died aged 11.

Wilfred was exempted from Army service until 1st October 1917 by the Bideford rural tribunal. He had applied for exemption on two grounds that seem to contradict each other. Firstly his representative suggested that it was amazing that he had been passed class A medically as he suffered from neurasthenia, neuritis and muscular rheumatism and had to rest after short periods of exercise. The former disease refers to mechanical weakness of the actual nerves causing fatigue, anxiety, headache,

The Family of Wilfred Davey - almost certainly Wilfred Davey far right

neuralgia and depression. The second is inflammation of the nerves causing impaired sensation, reflexes and strength, and with the rheumatic problem presumably affecting his muscles and joints he would appear a sorry specimen . On the other hand his father was the only other mason in the area and they were so busy working mainly on agricultural properties that his father could not possibly spare him even though he was so obviously handicapped he would appear to have not been a lot of use. Robert also replied to a question that he had not advertised for any additional masons as there was no-one to get! The Chairman said that he had had a leak in his roof for two years and he still had not managed to get it repaired due to the lack of tradesmen available. Wilfred was given a short period of exemption before joining up.

His case supports the belief that, although all families did not want their loved ones to go to war, for many the departure of young men put a great strain on their family businesses and caused substantial numbers of others to fold completely. He was eventually enlisted, probably late in 1917, and served as Private 462717 in the 2nd Connaught Rangers and on the absent voters list for spring 1919 he is recorded as being in the 621st Agricultural Company Labour corps.

He married Isabel Dark on 26th July 1920 and their son Trevor George was born in 1924. Wilfred died aged 68 in 1960.

Thomas Richard Headon

Thomas was born on 18th April 1891 in Hartland where he attended school. He was the son of Richard, a sailor of the seas, and Elizabeth, and he was one of five children. The others were Henry Curtis born 1886, Elizabeth in 1889, John in 1893 and Mary three years later. One had died by 1911 but BMD records doesn't record which one. In that year Thomas was employed as a waggoner at Highworthy Farm.

Thomas joined the Royal Naval division as K14472 Stoker second class for eleven years clearly following his father's nautical background. He served at Vivid II which was the Navy barracks at Devonport. It was commissioned in 1890, and operated as a training unit until 1914. The base was renamed HMS Drake in 1934. His first ship was the *Lancaster* where he was promoted to Stoker 1st class. HMS *Lancaster* was one of 10 Monmouth-class armoured cruisers built for the Royal Navy in the first decade of the 20th century. Upon completion she was assigned to the 3rd Cruiser Squadron of the Mediterranean Fleet. She remained there until 1912 when she returned home to be placed in reserve.

Thomas then sailed on *Berwick*. This ship was another one of the 10 Monmouth-class armoured cruisers built for the Royal Navy in the first decade of the 20th century. She captured a German merchant ship shortly after World War I began during his time on board. The ship patrolled for German commerce raiders and escorted convoys for the war.

He then returning to Devonport in 1915 for three months before joining *Ajax* in October and became acting leading stoker, then ten months later his role was made permanent.

HMS *Ajax* was a King George V-class battleship (one of four ships of the class), built at Scotts' shipyard at Greenock on the River Clyde. She was completed in 1913 and saw action at the Battle of Jutland in 1916 during his time on board. The following year, still on *Ajax*, he was again promoted to Acting Stoker Petty Officer then in March 1918 he returned to base in a similar role. In May his role as an officer was made permanent and he spent twelve months on HMS *Blenheim* before returning once more to Devonport for three months. HMS *Blenheim* was a Blake class, first class protected cruiser that served in the Royal Navy from 1890–1926. She was built by Thames Ironworks & Shipbuilding Company at Leamouth, London. The ship was named after the Battle of Blenheim. She served as a cruiser with the Channel Squadron until May 1908 when she joined the Mediterranean Fleet as a destroyer depot ship. She was sent to Mudros in March 1915 in support of the Mediterranean Expeditionary Force at the Battle of Gallipoli, which is where Thomas must have heard that the armistice had been signed. He finally embarked on *Columbine*, a three-masted steam-engined sloop of war built in the previous century, for the last months of his service which he completed on 30th July 1921.

He had a varied time in his naval career of nine years, almost half of that time in war situation and the rest in peace time. He certainly saw action.

A Richard T Headon married Florence Prouse in Spring 1918 which coincides with one of his periods at Devonport. They had a son, Frank, in 1921 and a daughter, Joan, a year later. Florence died in 1963 aged 82.

Edward Peard

Edward Peard was born early in 1884 at Alwington. His parents were William, a farm labourer, and Elizabeth née Glover. The family later moved to Woolsery village. The other children of their marriage were Mary born in 1874, Ann in 1875, Sarah a year later, Giles 1878, William 1882 then Charles in 1886, Alice in 1889 and the youngest John, who also served, in 1890.

Edward's occupation was listed as a farm labourer. He married Lilian Buse late in 1904 and their son William was born in 1906, with Reginald, Lilian Herbert James and Jesse all born in successive years. Other children of the union included Lesley born in 1912 and Leonard in 1913. He served as 248976 Driver in the Royal Field Artillery and was awarded the Victory and British War medals.

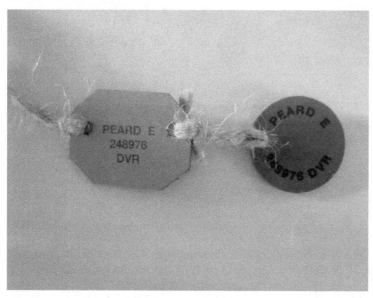

John Short

John was born in 1881 in Woolsery, his parents William Henry and Mary Sarah née Perkins lived at North Stroxworthy at the time of his birth. He was the third of three brothers; William was three years older and Edward one. They also had a younger sister Emily who was born in 1882. William, and later John, were always listed as farm labourers.

In 1904 John was in Alcester Warwickshire seven miles from Stratford-on-Avon where he married Harriet Sophia Davies who had been born in Lydbury North in Shropshire. What made their paths cross is lost in time, but they returned to be living at East View Cottage, Bucks Cross in 1911 with their only child Mabel who had been born the year before. She grew up to marry Herbert, son of Percy Thomas - another war hero - and Stuart Thomas is their grandson.

John attested on 29th December 1916 as Private 227998 and was mobilised two days later with the Royal Engineers. A month later he embarked for France and in November 1917 was promoted to Lance Corporal, four months later he was to became a Sapper. At this time Sappers were often the brave men who dug trenches ever closer to enemy lines and in some cases actually tunnelled to undermine enemy gun posts and other strategic positions.

On 26th June 1919, he was demobilised as a Lance Corporal and was recorded as still living at East View where he joined Harriet and Mabel. He is remembered in later life as having lived at Pleadymead and then Myrtle Cottage, currently the home of the editor of this present volume. He was awarded the Victory and British Army medals and died 26th April 1949 in Exeter aged 68, Harriet dying ten years later aged 75.

William Glover

William was the son of Edward and Thirza Glover of Huddisford, Woolsery. He was born in 1883. He was one of a family of eight with five brothers John, Samuel, Frederick, Ernest and George and two sisters Emma and Annie. Their father was a farmer and when William started work he began as a "carter on farm agriculture horse" but by 1911 was an engine driver tractor, still working on the family farm, so he clearly saw where the revolution in agriculture was going.

In the final quarter of 1905 he had two major events in his life. Firstly he married his neighbour Elizabeth Grace Boundy who was five years his senior. When they had only been married for a few weeks, she died aged just thirty. Seven years later he married another local girl, Elison Brent, daughter of Reuben and Ann. They had at least two children William G in 1913 and Betty in 1921. He served in the Devon Yeomanry and it is reported that he took his own horse to war. His granddaughter Loye Medd still lives in the village.

Charles Peard

Charles Peard was born early in 1886 at Alwington and was the brother of Edward above. His parents were William, a farm labourer, and Elizabeth née Glover. The family later moved to Woolsery village, having moved around the locality quite often, with their children listed as having been born in various villages. The other children of their marriage were Mary born in 1874, Ann in 1875, Sarah a year later, Giles 1878, William 1882 then Edward 1884 Charles in 1886, Alice in 1889 and the youngest John who also served in 1890.

Charles worked as a "cow boy cattle agricultural labourer" at Lane Barton, Woolsery in 1901 and ten years later was a horseman on a farm at Braunton, he married Annie M. Cook in 1912 , who was a Sunday school teacher. Before he left for war service he moved back to Woolsery living at Greenaway Cottage, currently the home of Margaret Rickard. He enlisted with Richard Moore who lived next door at the top of Back Street. When they departed Mrs Moore moved in with Mrs Peard and didn't return home when the men were demobbed. Mrs Peard must have been more hospitable than she was to some evacuees who were billeted with her in the following war and to whom she showed little kindness.

Charles served as a private soldier 15073 in the 2nd battalion of the Devon Regiment shown on manoeuvres above. He was twice wounded - in May 1915 and August 1916 - but survived and was awarded the Victory Medal, British War Medal and 1915 Star. The latter proved that he volunteered prior to conscription, which was introduced with the British Military Act of 1916.

William Lewis Boundy

William Boundy was the son of William and Ann Boundy who farmed at Cross Park in Bradworthy where he was born. His father was Woolsery born and his mother was born in Hartland. The other children of the family were Selina Ann and Emmeline who were older, and Frances, Katherine, Mary and John born after William. Ann, their mother, died shortly after John's birth aged just 41. The family continued at the farm then moved to another farm at West Putford.

William enrolled in the in the 1st/6th Battalion Devon Regiment (Territorial) as private 2616. A company of this Battalion is pictured here during a well-earned rest. He died on 20th November 1916 in Mesopotamia fighting against the Ottoman Empire. His memorial is at Kirkee India. At his death he is recorded as the son of Mr and Mrs William Boundy of Cranford House, Woolsery. It appears that William Senior had retired, remarried and moved back to his birthplace.

This one was almost in the parish and remembered at Clovelly

William Stevens

The Hartland and West Country Chronicle of September 1917 reported the death in France of Lance Corporal William Stevens son of Mr William Stevens, a waggoner, of Burscott and formerly Mouth Mill. Another son was serving in India. William jnr. had only returned from leave two weeks previously. A letter received from his commanding officer explained the circumstances of his death.

Dear Mr Stevens

I am sure you will have heard of your poor son William Stevens being killed in action on the 16th inst. As I was sitting close to him when he was hit, I thought you would like to hear from me. We were just digging into a shell hole and your son was hit in the neck by a sniper. He was killed instantaneously and had no pain at all.

I have been in your son's section for over twelve months now and I have always found him such a splendid fellow. He was very brave and always cheerful. He was loved by every man in his section and his loss will be greatly felt by us all.

Please accept my deepest sympathy in your sad loss. I should have written to you before but I was hit in the right shoulder less than an hour after your son was killed.

Believe me yours faithfully

Sidney Edeens
2nd Lieutenant
100th M.G. Company

His mother was Angelina and he had four siblings: John, presumably the son who was in India at the time of William's demise, Mary, James and Daniel. William had enlisted in the 11th Devons in September 1915 and was trained at Wareham before he sailed for France at the beginning of February 1916. There he was attached to a machine gun section. Since leaving school and until he enlisted he had lived and worked for his uncle, Daniel Stevens, at Fords Farm, Bradworthy.

EVERY GIRL PULLING
FOR VICTORY

VICTORY

VICTORY GIRLS
UNITED WAR WORK CAMPAIGN

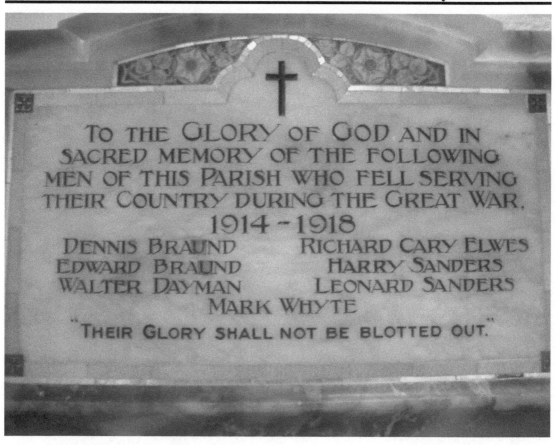

To the Glory of God and in Sacred Memory of the following men of this Parish who fell serving their country during the Great War, 1914 - 1918

DENNIS BRAUND   RICHARD CARY ELWES
EDWARD BRAUND   HARRY SANDERS
WALTER DAYMAN   LEONARD SANDERS
            MARK WHYTE

"Their Glory Shall Not Be Blotted Out."

Men from Bucks Cross and Bucks Mills

Charles Frederick (Charlie) Braund

Charlie Braund was born in 1884 at 8 Bucks Mills, and died in 1943 aged 59 years.

His parents were Frederick and Elizabeth Ann Braund née Crews. He married Eliza W Davey in 1919 and they had a son Grenville C Braund born in 1921. They lived in 'The Temperance Hotel' (now the Old Mill) at Bucks Mills and his occupation was a shop keeper and rabbit trapper. He was one of eleven and his siblings were Henry, Minnie, Beatrice, Ethel, Frederick, Isabella, Charlotte, Carrie, Emily and Theodore.

Charlie was attested as 39000 Pte in the Royal North Devon Hussars on 18th December 1912. He completed annual training in 1913 and 1914 and

was mobilised/home from 05 Aug 1914 – 14 Sep 1916. He was with M.E.F. (Mediterranean Expeditionary Force) from 15 Sep 1916 – 27 Dec 1918. He served in Salonika and Egypt and was hospitalised on 16th Apr 1917 due to an injury to his right hip and 18th Jan 1919 due to dysentery. He was recorded as on route to UK on 28th Dec 1918. He became a member of the Old Comrades Association at Barnstaple and served in the Home Guard in WW2.

Dennis Braund

Dennis Braund was born in 1881 at 7 Bucks Mills. He was one of five children: Frank, (Dennis), Cecil, Mark and Hilda. His parents were James and Elizabeth Braund née Steer.

He enlisted in Bideford and served as Corporal 9667 1st Battalion Devonshire regiment. He died of his wounds on 17th May 1915, age 24 in Salford District, Lancashire. He is buried in Bucks Mills Church Cemetery and was posthumously awarded the Victory Medal, the British War Medal and 1914 Star.

His brother Mark served in the Royal Navy and did return home safely.

North Devon Journal 29.04.1915
'Pte Dennis Braund native of Bucks Mills Parkham is reported to have been severely wounded in both arms.'

North Devon Journal 10.05.1915
'Pte Dennis Braund native of Parkham died in hospital on Tues from wounds received in action.'

Edward Braund

Edward Braund was born on 7th April 1898 at Bucks Mills. His parents were Arthur James and Lavinia Braund née Braund. He was one of six and his siblings were Herbert, Miriam, Harold, Agnes and James.

He enlisted 22nd May 1916 and was assigned to the Devonport shore base *Vivid II*. From Aug 1916 Edward was a stoker 2nd class on HMS *King Alfred*, Royal Navy. HMS *King Alfred* was one of four Drake-class armoured cruisers built for the Royal Navy around 1900. She served as flagship of the China Station from 1906 until relieved in 1910. Upon her return home that year, she was placed in reserve before being recommissioned in mid-1914. She was assigned to the 6th Cruiser Squadron of the Grand Fleet at the beginning of World War I. She was transferred to the 9th Cruiser Squadron in 1915 and assigned to convoy protection duties by the end of the year. She participated in the unsuccessful

searches for the German commerce raider SMS *Möwe* in 1916–17 before beginning to escort convoys later that year. The ship was torpedoed by a German submarine in 1918, but returned to service. She was sold for scrap in 1920.

Edward Braund, whose home is shown above, was allocated service number was K/33252 and he died 16th Sept 1916 in Royal Naval Hospital in Gibraltar from pneumonia. He is commemorated in Gibraltar North Front Cemetery Grave C. 3387, where 651 men are remembered.

Joseph Braund

Joseph Braund was born on 1st June 1893 at Woolsery and died 16th April 1975 in Bideford aged 82. His parents were Ernest and Regina Maud Braund née Braund. In 1911 he was living with mother Maud and sister Mary at Corner Cottage (Bucks Cliff). It is assumed that his father Ernest, a fisherman, was at sea. Joseph had a sister Mary E Braund. On 26th May 1915 in the District of Bideford he married Ethel Jane Smale; they had a son Morris who died as a baby and then Stella who was born in 1918. Joseph lived at Laburnham Cottage (left) at Bucks Mills. Stella is the

Grandmother of Darren Powell of Woolsery & Sarah Johns of Woolsery and now Hartland. Sarah's daughter Sophie was one of the ATC cadets who read the roll call in the church on the Woolsery WW1 Centenary day. Joseph's war service was at sea on HM Transport "Aysgarth" in 1919.

Mark Braund

Mark Braund was born on the 25th September 1896 at 7 Bucks Mills, he died 9th May 1969 in the District of Bideford.

He was one of five children: Frank, Dennis (died at war), Cecil, (Mark) and Hilda. He attended the Council School of Clovelly and in 1916 received a prize for 98% attendance. His parents were James and Elizabeth Braund née Steer.

In 1928 he married Sarah Gillett and they had two children: Noel W born 1930 and Dennis J born 1933. Kaye Braund-Phillips and her sister Lorraine are his granddaughters.

He served in the Royal Navy Service Number K31472.

Vivid II Sto II
06 Mar 1916 – 07 May 1916
Princetown Sto II
08 May 1916 – 30 Sep 1916
Mars   Sto II
10 Sep 1916

Mars   Sto I
06 Mar 1917 – 17 Aug 1917
Vivid IISto I
18 Aug 1917 – 06 Sep 1917
ApolloSto I
07 Sep 1917 – 24 Feb 1919
Demobilised

William George Braund

William Braund was born in 1872 in Woolsery and died 1st July 1932 in Bideford Hospital aged 60 years. His parents were Joseph and Ann Elizabeth Braund née Fry. In 1908 he married Isabella Fry in Wellington, New Zealand, but sadly she died later that year.

He went on to marry Mabel Stephenson in Lancaster, Lancashire in 1912. His siblings were Charles A, Maria J, Ada Mary and Ernest. William, like many of the Bucks and Clovelly men , was a seaman and on 5th April 1894 received the "Second Mates" Certificate, 21st November 1895 received "Mates" Certificate and 16th Oct 1897 received "Masters" Certificate. He was awarded Mercantile Marine Medal and British War Medal. William Braund retired from the sea in about 1927 due to poor health and was then associated with his wife in the management of *Bucks Cliff Hotel*. He was a member of Bideford Lodge of Freemasons.

Joseph Carter

Joesph Carter lived at Church Park Farm, Bucks Cross and served as 7676 Pte Royal Irish Regiment and then transferred as 92643 Pte Liverpool Regiment. He was on active service in France from 11th January 1915 and awarded the Victory Medal, British War Medal and 1915 Star.

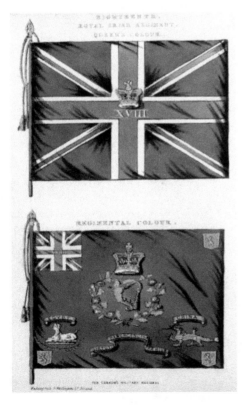

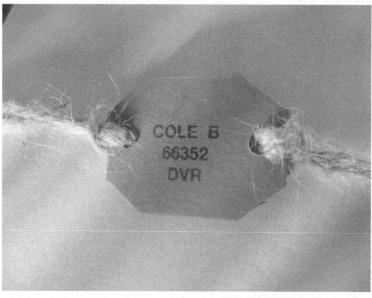

Bert Cole

He was born 2nd July 1897 and attended Woolsery Primary School. His parents are recorded as Edward Cole (address Stroxworthy). His home is recorded as Church Park Farm and Walland Cottage, Bucks Cross

He served as 66352 Dvr. 21st Bat M.G.C. (Machine Gun Corps) and was awarded Victory Medal and British War Medal. A Machine Gun Corps unit with their Vickers gun is pictured above.

Ernest Cole

Is on the absent voters list and he lived at Walland Cottage, Bucks. Ernest and Bert could have been brothers, but we have found no further details on them.

William Cudmore

William Cudmore lived at Bucks Cross and his service details are 246622 PTE. 445th Ag. Co. L.

Because we know so little about these two men, we thought it appropriate here to remember the men about whom we know nothing at all. During the First World War, the British and French armies who were allies during the war jointly decided to bury soldiers themselves. In Britain, under the Imperial War Graves Commission (now Commonwealth War Graves Commission), the Reverend David Railton had seen a grave marked by a rough cross while serving in the British Army as a chaplain on the Western Front, which bore the pencil-written legend "An Unknown British Soldier".

He suggested (together with the French in their own country) the creation at a national level of a symbolic funeral and burial of an "Unknown Warrior", proposing that the grave should in Britain include a national monument in the form of what is usually, but not in this particular case, a headstone. The idea received the support of the Dean of Westminster, Prime Minister David Lloyd George, and later from King George V, responding to a wave of public support. In this picture Field Marshal Douglas Haig and Field Marshall John French, first Earl of Ypres, walked beside the coffin of the Unknown Warrior as it was carried in procession from Victoria station to the Cenotaph.

John Wesley Dark

John Dark was born in September 1892 in Woolsery, he died 23 Jul 1954 at Royal Devon and Exeter Hospital, living at Lynfield, Sticklepath, Barnstaple.

He attended Woolsery Primary School and appears to be in the care of Wm Crocker at the hotel, which we believe to be the *Farmers Arms*. His parents were James and Mary Ann Dark née Ching. James died Sep qtr 1907 in district of Bideford. In 1911 John was living in Bucks Cross Post Office. He married Eliza Jane Bond in Sep qtr 1920 in the district of Bideford. They had two children Jean & Ron. He was one of nine and his siblings were: Dennis, Ada M, William J, Gilbert, Sidney R, Isabel, (John Wesley), Hettie and Rosalie Hevlyn. He served as 202486 Pte in 12th Bn. Oxford and Bucks.

11.12.1915	Attested, to Army Reserve.
06.06.1916	Mobilised as Pte.
08 05. 1916	Posted to 12th Bn. Oxford and Bucks.
15.06 1918	Missing, P.O.W. in Austria.
07.12.1918	Repatriated
03.03.1919	Demobilised.

Awarded Victory Medal and British War Medal

Charlie and Harry Davey
The father and son who went to war as horse men

Charlie Davey

Charlie Davey was born in 1869 and died in 1944. He is buried in the upper church yard Bucks Cross in an unmarked grave. He married Mary Beer who died in childbirth in 1896, and later married Evelina Dark. Charlie Davey is reported as living at a cottage at West Bucks Whitehouse Farm, lodging with Lucy Braund.

He served as 799 CPL R.L.N. DEVON. (HRS.) I.Y. (Royal North Devon (Hussars), Imperial Yeomanry *) and received a rare long service and good conduct medal which is in the hands of his great grandson John Luckett of Wembsworthy, Hartland. Another medal which is his has 'The Nile 1884-85' engraved on a bar above the medal and 'Egypt' on the medal.

* Ian Arnold has clarified some of the abbreviations as there is some confusion about this. The mounted cavalry soldiers were variously known as; NDH North Devon Hussars, RNDH Royal North Devon Hussars, NDY North Devon Yeomanry and RNDY Royal North Devon Yeomanry. In the case of Charlie Davey, Ian believes he is likely to be RL. N. DEVON (HRS). I.Y. which is Royal North Devon (Hussars), Imperial Yeomanry. The Imperial part reflects that they served in South Africa.

Henry ('Harry') Davey

Harry Davey was born in 1896 and sadly his mother Mary Beer died during his birth. He had an elder sister Eliza Mary known as 'Lowe', who was two years older than him and they were brought up by Melinda Jones at Bucks Mills, who had two sons. Lowe worked in Bucks Mills shop which was owned by her son Grenvill & Edith Braund. Harry Davey attended Halwell School near the *Hoops Inn*. Harry died on 17th October 1978, and is buried in the upper churchyard at Bucks Cross in an unmarked grave.

Harry Davey served as 39019 Pte. Devon Regiment and then transferred as 12194 Pte. South Wales Borderers and later transferred as 20372 Pte. 2nd Connaught Rangers. He was awarded the Victory Medal and British War Medal.

Harry Davey is the grandfather of John Luckett of Wembsworthy, Hartland, who recalls that both Harry and his father Charlie went to war together as horsemen, taking messages. They both returned from war and were thrashing contractors. Charlie is remembered as a 'wild man' in his day!

Walter Thomas Dayman

Walter Dayman was born in 1883 at Bucks Cross. His parents were John Henry & Mary Jane Dayman née Curtis.

He married Bessie Jane Dayman née Blythe of South view, Holcombe Rogus, Wellington, Somerset. Walter is a native of Hartland, Devon.

He enlisted in Exeter and served as PTE 203572 4th (Reserve) Battalion (Territorials) Devonshire Regiment and died 2nd March 1917 aged 33 in Christchurch District Dorset. He is buried in Bournemouth East Cemetery Grave P.I. 146.

Richard Cary Elwes

Strangely there are no military or other records found for Richard Elwes. Local information confirms that he was the son of Philip Francis Cary Elwes and Hester Lucy née Pinney, the owner of the Walland Estate. He was a very wealthy man who owned Walland Estate which contained most of Bucks and a large part of Woolsery parish including West Town Farm, Ashcroft and Clifford. Walland Cary is now known as Bideford Bay Holiday Park.

Born 1891 in Somerton, Somerset he attended Moat House College, Wraxall, Somerset. He left the country in 1912 for Mozambique. There is a report of his death on 21st Nov 1914 but it doesn't seem to be anything to do with the war so we are unsure why his name appears on the memorial.

The Hartland Gazette on 22.12.1914 reports that 'Mr & Mrs Elwes of Somerton Somerset and Walland Cary, have received news of the death of their only son R.C.H. Elwes in Rhodesia, Mr Elwes is said to have been murdered by natives.'

The lectern in St Anne's Church, Bucks Mills is engraved 'To the Glory of God and in memory of Richard Henry Lincoln Cary Elwes killed in S.A. Nov 21 1914'

Fredrick H Jenkins

Fredrick was on the spring 1919 absent voters list and lived at Bucks Cross.

John Johns

John Johns lived at Walland

Cottage, Bucks Cross.

He served as 267186 Pte. 2/6th Devon Regiment and was awarded the Victory Medal and British War Medal.

Frederick William Johns

Frederick Johns was born 21st May 1892 at Maids Moor, Woolsery, he died Sep qtr 1990 in District of Okehampton. He attended Woolsery Primary School. His parents were James Thomas and Athaliah Johns née Short, of the Village (this probably means Woolsery Village). The Spring 1919 absent voters list places his next of kin at Bucks Cross. He was one of eight children: (Frederick William), Maria, Margaret Mary Grace, Franklin Albert John, William Stanley, Gilbert and Olive Irene.

He attested as Pte 905 Royal North Devon (Yeoman) and was transferred to Pte 345585 6th Devon Regt. (Yeomany). He was in the theatre of war from 29 September 1915 and was awarded the Victory Medal, the British War Medal and 1915 Star.

Walter Thomas Johns

Walter Johns was born 23rd November 1896 in Burford, Clovelly and died 8th February 1987 in Bideford and District Hospital. He may have been known as William. Siblings : Frederick William, Maria, Margaret Mary Grace, Franklin Albert John, William Stanley, Gilbert and Olive Irene. He attended Woolsery Primary School and is recorded there as Walter John Johns with parent Thomas and an address of Stroxwothy.

His parents were James Thomas and Athaliah Johns née Short. On 8th May 1920 he married Mary Florence Prouse in the United Methodist Church, Hartland. They had three children: Fernley Walter, Stanley William, Freda Eileen. The absent voters list places his next of kin at South Down Cottage, Bucks Cross.

AUSTRALIAN WAR MEMORIAL   H08925

He was attested as 280137 Pte 332 R.C. Coy. R.E. (Railway construction company, Royal Engineers), seen above in this picture from the Royal Australian War Memorial.

21.05.1917   Mobilised
12.06 1917   Embarked BEF (British Expeditionary Force which usually refers to the first soldiers sent to France)
30.11.1917   Re-mustered Sapper Engine Driver "Steam Roller" Proficient.
27.08.1918   Loss of 4 days pay for being absent without leave for 1 day when on active service.
07.10.1918   Raised to Skilled Rate of SP.
20.11.1919   Demobilised.
He was awarded the Victory Medal and British War Medal.

The Spring 1919 Absent Voters List records that he was WR/24311 SPR 5th Army Road Workshops R.E. (Royal Engineers)

Walter Thomas Johns is Brenda Pennington's grandfather, and was a brother to Fredrick William Johns, and they were both council workers driving steam wagons, and later lorries. Walter Thomas lived from 1896-1987.

John Edward Pickard

John Pickard was born June qtr 1876 at Parkham and died 19th December 1930 at Bucks Cross. His parents were John and Mary Gorvin Pickard née Punchard. He had two sisters Emily A and Susanna.

In the March qtr of 1899 he married Huldah Davey in the district of Bideford. They had a son, Edward George born 1871 and a daughter. In the 1911 Census, John was working as a waggoner on a farm at Cullamartin, Instow. Huldah was visiting William Moore and family at West Moor, Woolsery.

He served as 44680 Pte. 1/19 London.

North Devon Journal 01 Jan 1931: There was a large attendance at the funeral at Woolsery West on Monday the 22nd inst., at the funeral of Mr. John E Pickard, a well known farmer of Bucks Cross, who died after a brief illness in his 56th year, leaving a widow and a son and daughter, who were both married.

Mr Pickard had taken an active part in the life of the Alminstone Wesleyan Church, and was for several years Superintendent of the Sunday School there. Prior to the burial a service was conducted at the house by Mr. C Harding and Mr. E Dunn, and at the Church Yard by the Revs E L Lewis (Woolsery) and Guy S Whittaker (Bucks Cross) officiated. Before going to Bucks Cross to farm, Mr. Pickard was a member of the Wesleyan choir of Parkham, an enthusiastic bell ringer and a member of the Parkham Village band.."

Harry Sanders

Harry Saunders who was also known as Henry was born in 1892 at 15 Bucks Mills. His parents were James Henry and Emily Sanders née Braund (pictured opposite) who had four children all of whom died. Harry's siblings were his brother Leonard who also lost his life to the war and Hettie & Oswald who died as babies. He served as

Cadet 138312 8th Cadet Wing, Royal Air Force, and died on the 8th March 1919, buried on 12th March at Bucks Mills.

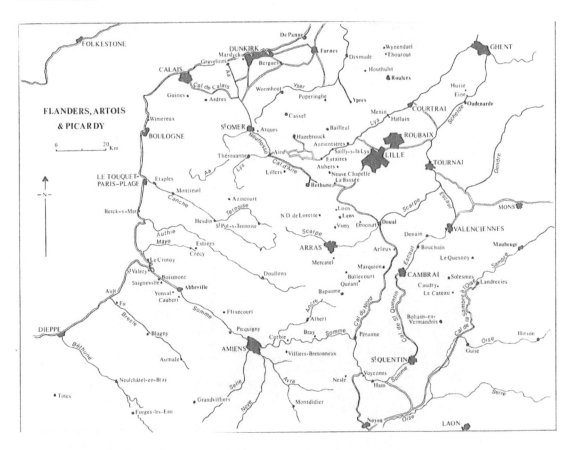

Leonard Sanders

Leonard Sanders was born in 1892 at 15 Bucks Mills.

His parents were James Henry and Emily Sanders née Braund who had four children all of whom died. Leonard's siblings were his brother Harry who also lost his life to the war and Hettie & Oswald who died as babies. He enlisted in Barnstaple and served as 2193 R.N.D. Hussars and then PTE 20371 5th Battalion Connaught Rangers. He was killed in action in Flanders 8th Nov 1918.

Age 23 he was involved in the march to victory in Picardy and Artois. He is commemorated on panel 10 Vis En Artois Memorial Pas De Calais France where 9,833 men are remembered, and he is commemorated Bucks Mills.

Hartland & West Country Chronicle 29.11.1918:

> 'The news has been received with much regret of the death in action in France on
> Nov. 8th, of Lance Corporal L. Saunders Connaught Rangers, son of Mr & Mrs J
> Sanders, and formally assistant gamekeeper on the Walland Cary Estate. He joined

the R.N.D. Hussars in October 1914, and had served in Salonica and Egypt as well as in France. A brother has also been serving since 1914. Sympathy is felt with the parents, and with Miss Melinda Braund, of Bucks Mills, to whom the deceased gallant soldier was engaged to be married.'

Alfred Thorne

Alfie Thorne was born on 20th May 1892 in Hartland. He died on 17th June 1973 in the district of Barnstaple. His parents were Richard and Mary Lizzie Thorne née Cook. In the September qtr 1910 he married Florrie Cann in the district of Bideford. They had a daughter, Ivy Elizabeth born 1924, but she died in 1926; they then had four children: Tilly (Matilda) Mary, Alice Susan (the mother of Colin Stevens of Alminstone), Charlie Thorne (of Hartland) and Dorothy Rose (of Welcombe). He was one of four and his siblings were: Eliza, Richard and Frederick. On 10th May 1916 he attested as 332873 15th O/S Brigade Canadian Field Artillery (CFA), previous trade fireman, address No1 Firehall, Victoria, BC. Next of kin, mother Mary Vanstone of Burford Farm, Woolsery.

Local people remember Alfie well and have reported that he went to Canada, Lived at Number 2 Cross Cottage on return and then was at Pick Park (Oakapple Cottage) before renting South Stroxworthy from Tom Cann, his brother-in-law from 1946-1958, he then went to Cranford where he lived until he died.

From his photograph you can see he had one injury stripe on his uniform.

Alfie Thorne's son Charlie of Hartland remembers:

Alfie was born at Burford and later rented South Stroxworthy Farm. He went to Canada as a young man to see his sister (Elliza) who lived there. He first worked in a logging camp (about 1910) and then for the Fire brigade before he joined the Canadian Army to fight in WW1. On joining the Canadian Army he was questioned about his Christian denomination as he had to be Church of England in order to represent the country and serve in the Army!

Alfie fought in the battle of Vimy Ridge when the Germans were up high taking easy aim at the allies. The Canadians went around the back and squeezed the Germans out. He was involved in the battle at Mons firing artillery guns, it was using an artillery gun that he became injured (indicated by an injury stripe on his uniform), as the gun fired it rolled back onto his big toe breaking it. This type of injury was referred to by the soldiers as a

**NOTE—This Certificate is to be issued without any altera-
tions in the manuscript.**

Certificate of discharge of No. 332873 Rank... Dvr.

Name... Thorne   Alfred.
       Surname.   Christian Names in full.

Unit*
and
Regiment or Corps   C.F.A.
from which discharged
* The unit of the Regiment or Corps such as Field Co. R.E., H.T., or M.T., A.S.C., etc.,
is invariably to be stated.

Regiment or Corps to which first posted... C.F.A.

Also previously served in.....................................

....

....

MILITARY CHARACTER   **VERY GOOD**

Only Regiments or Corps in which the soldier served since August 4th, 1914, are to be
stated. If inapplicable this space is to be ruled through in ink and initialled.

Specialist Qualifications (Military).....................................

....

Medals, Clasps,   [* France 1917
Decorations and   ....   Wound Stripes* Nil
Mentions in dispatches [.....................   To be inserted in words.

Has served Overseas on Active Service†

Enlisted at... Victoria B.C. ....on... May 4 ...191
   *Each space is to be filled in and the word "nil" inserted where necessary.
       †To be struck out in ink if not applicable.

He is discharged in consequence of... K. R. & O. Para. 392 Sec. XXV
.... (Being Demobilized in England—C.R.O. 5222)

after serving* Three ...years* 106 ...days with the Colours, and
.......✓...years.......✓...days in the   Army Reserve } Strike out
                        or   } whichever
                   Territorial Force† } inapplicable.
*Each space is to be filled in and the word "nil" inserted where necessary; number of
years to be written in words.
†Service with Territorial Force to be shown only in cases of soldiers serving on a
T.F. attestation.

Date of discharge.....................   Signature
23-8-19   J. V. Mackreynolds: Capt.

Officer i/c No 2 C.D.D. Records.
         London (Place).

Description of the above-named soldier when he left the Colours.

Year of Birth... 1882 ..... Marks or Scars...
Height... 5 ..ft. 7 ...in.
Complexion... Dark.
Eyes... Brown ...Hair... Black

WARNING.—If this Certificate is lost a duplicate cannot be issued. You should therefore on no account part with it or forward it by post when applying for a situation.

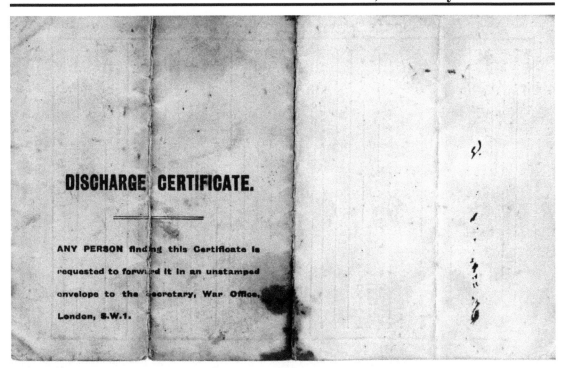

cushy, that is when a soldier receives a minor injury which permitted them a break from duty (The Trench, Trevor York 2014).

During his time in Belgium, Alfie came across a cottage where he met some twins; the Germans had killed their parents and left them to fend for themselves. Alfie acquired and came home with a photo of these twins. Alfie also came across a German who he thought was dead; he had on a tin helmet. Alfie went to retrieve the hat from the German's head, but as he did so the German opened his eyes and asked Alfie for a cigarette. Alfie obliged and the German gave him a photo of his wife and two daughters, which Alfie passed on and it got returned to his family. The German died in Alfie's arms.

Alfie was carrying messages to the front when his horse was hit by a 'Whizz banger' (a German shell); he survived but his horse did not. He received two medals although the whereabouts of them is not known. On return from the war he returned to Woolsery and farmed. He was good at calving cows and would operate on pigs. He gave his tools to the local vet, David Hobbs. He also served in WW2 with the home guards, guarding Common Moor and Thorne Moor.

Colin Stevens remembers his mum (Alfie's daughter) telling him:

My mother told me that Alfie had overstayed his leave and the military police came for him. He was digging potatoes in the garden at South Stroxworthy and saw them coming up the lane. He ran up across the field and into the house telling his mother that he is in bed ill. They knocked on the door and she sent them up to him. When they came down they said 'indeed he does seem to be running a temperature, send him when he is well.'

Information from Wendy Burrow (Alfie's granddaughter) collected from Canada military war archives:

Medical records show he had mumps and was admitted to Aldershot Isolation on 6th March 1917 and was discharged on 26th March 1917. It looks like he had not been on active service before this but in England training. When he returned home, like lots of the soldiers he had lice and dysentery.

He joined the Canadian Expeditionary Forces on May 10th 1916 at Victoria B.C. in Canada as a means of passage home and he was discharged on 23rd Aug 1919. He embarked from Halifax Canada 11.09.16 travelling on the SS *Cameronia,* then disembarked England Liverpool 22.09.16.

He moved batteries a number of times but details included are:

Service number: 332873
Ranks include: Gunner, Driver
62nd Battery 15th O/S Brigade C.F.A

13th Brigade 51st Battery C.F.A requested to move to 10th brigade C.F.A of the 35th battery C.F.A for the purpose of accompanying Captain Carmichail as groom, aged 24 and 310 days.
51st Battery New 13 Brigade
Transferred to 13th Brigade
Granted leave to UK 16.09.18 to 10.10.18

James Thorne

James Thorne was born on 26th Feb 1892 at Bucks Mills, he joined the R.N.D. (Royal Naval Division; sailors who because they had no ship served as soldiers) as K31477 Sto II., he was previously a farm labourer.

Vivid II	Sto II	06.03.1916	–
07.05.1916			
Princetown	Sto II	08.05.1916	–
30.12.1916			
Mars	Sto II	01 10.1916	
Mars	Sto I	06 .03.1917	–

17.08.1917

Vivid II	Sto I	18.08.1917 – 03.11.1917
Blake (Mystic)	Sto I	04.11.1917 – 20.03.1918
Hecla (Mystic)	Sto I	21.03.1918 – 31.03.1918
Leander (Mystic)	Sto I	01.04.1918 – 30.04.1918
Hecla (Mystic)	Sto I	01.03.1918 – 20.12.1918
Vivid II	Sto I	21.12.1918 – 07.03.1919 Demobilised

Mark Gilchrist Whyte

Mark Gilchrist Whyte was born in 1898 in St Andrews, Fife.

His parents were Theodore George William and Maude Josepha Whyte née Ogilvy of Whyte Cottage, Bucks Mills; they married in Colorado. He was one of four and his siblings were: Madeline Josephine, Felix, Maryott Honoria (who was a nanny to Winston Churchill's children).

He served as 2nd Lieutenant 2nd Battalion Royal Fusiliers, he was gazetted as temporary 2nd Lieutenant 28 March 1917 and died 19th Aug 1918 age 20. He is remembered with honour at Borre British Cemetery Nord Grave II.H.16, France where 365 casualties are remembered, and at the war memorial at Blundells School, Tiverton (pictured here) where he was a pupil.

William Grant Woolrich.   20th   Apr.
1917.

The undermentioned to be Lts. 19th Apr.
1917 :—
Clement Clapton Chesterman, from Bristol
Univ. Cont., O.T.C.
Joseph Clinton Collins.

———

War Office,
8th May, 1917.

REGULAR FORCES.

INFANTRY.
R. W. Surr. R.
Cadet Norman Stanley Ford to be temp.
2nd Lt. (attd.).   28 Mar. 1917.

E. Kent R.
The undermentioned cadets to be temp.
2nd Lts. (attd.) :—
28 Mar. 1917.
Harry James Harris.
Theodore Overy.

R. Lanc. R.
The undermentioned cadets to be temp.
2nd Lts. (attd.) :—
28 Mar. 1917.
John Arthur Edgar Roche.
George Hemmant.

North'd Fus.
The undermentioned cadets to be temp.
2nd Lts. (attd.) :—
28 Mar. 1917.
William Edwin Dwelley.
David Evans.
Ridley Martin Hall.
Percy Gerald Lambert.
Geoffrey Sheringham.
Letson Alfred Tavener.

R. War. R.
Temp. 2nd Lt. (attd.) J. C. Brown relin-
quishes his commission on account of ill-
health, and is granted the hon. rank of 2nd
Lt.   9 May, 1917.

R. Fus.
The undermentioned cadets to be temp.
2nd Lts. (attd.) :—
28 Mar. 1917.
Rae Bruce McCallum.
Cecil Henry Taylor.
Ronald Frank Tooley.
Mark Gilchrist Whyte.
Arthur Ernest Banti.
Herbert Edward Biggs.
Dudley Athelstan Beresford Fry.
Herbert Reeve.

Devon. R.
Cadet Charles Henry Cosway to be temp.
2nd Lt. (attd.).   28 Mar. 1917.

W. York. R.
Cadet John Fernyhough to be temp. 2nd
Lt. (attd.).   28 Mar. 1917.

E. York. R.
The undermentioned cadets to be temp.
2nd Lts. (attd.) :—
28 Mar. 1917.
Jackson Page.
Victor Lodovico Franzini.
Cecil Greenhalgh.

Bedf. R.
Cadet Joseph Richard Reynolds to be
temp. 2nd Lt. (attd.).   28 Mar 1917.

Leic. R.
The undermentioned cadets to be temp.
2nd Lts. (attd.) :—
28 Mar. 1917.
Douglas Henry Holland.
Ralph Alcock.

Lan. Fus.
Cadet Joseph Crookes Grime to be temp.
2nd Lt. (attd.).   25 Jan. 1917.   (Substi-
tuted for Gaz. notification of 10 Apr. 1917,
page 3410, incorrectly specifying date of
appt. as 1 Mar. 1917.)
Cadet Robert Nisbet to be temp. 2nd Lt.
(attd.).   28 Mar. 1917.

R.W. Fus.
Temp. Capt. T. H. Phipps, from a Res.
Bn., to be temp. Capt. (attd.).   20 Sept.
1916, with seniority from 31 Mar. 1915.

The undermentioned cadets to be temp.
2nd Lts. (attd.) :—
28 Mar. 1917.
John Harold Jones.
Thomas William Lewis.

Worc. R.
The undermentioned cadets to be temp.
2nd Lts. (attd.) :—
28 Mar. 1917.
Eric Mansfield Stuart.
Bertram Edward Tompson.

E. Surr. R.
Cadet Ernest Carpenter to be temp. 2nd
Lt. (attd.).   28 Mar. 1917.

D. of Corn. L.I.
Temp. Capt. R. F. Phillips, M.C., from
a Serv. Bn., to be temp. Capt. (attd.).
12 Feb. 1917 with seniority from 22 Nov.
1915.
Temp. Capt. (attd.) W. Andrews relin-
quishes his commission on account of ill-
health contracted on active service, and is
granted the hon. rank of Capt.   9 May 1917.

W. Rid. R.
The undermentioned cadets to be temp.
2nd Lts. (attd.) :—
28 Mar. 1917.
William Susman.
Charles David Jones.

R. Suss. R.
Temp. Capt. E. G. Cassels, from a Serv.
Bn., to be temp. Capt. (attd.).   12 Feb.
1917, with seniority from 27 Nov. 1914.
Cadet Charles Cecil Garner to be temp.
2nd Lt. (attd.).   28 Mar. 1917.

Hamps. R.
Temp. Lt. L. T. Wire, from a Serv. Bn.,
to be temp. Lt. (attd.).   4 Feb. 1917,
with seniority from 27 Mar. 1916.
Cadet Thomas Victor Walter Wallace to
be temp. 2nd Lt. (attd.).   28 Mar. 1917.

S. Staff. R.
Temp. 2nd Lt. M. Russell, from Linc. R.,
to be temp. 2nd Lt. (attd.).   14 Apr. 1917,
but with seniority from 7 Aug. 1915.

Dorset. R.
Temp. Maj. T. H. F. Johnson, D.S.O.,
from a Serv. Bn., to be temp. Maj. (attd.).

Arthur Shackson (born 01.03.46) of Auction Way, Woolsery remembers his father Arthur Shackson's war experiences.

by Jane Cann

Arthur Shackson was born 17th September 1895 and was the son of Charles Frederick Shackson and Mary Elizabeth née Dunn. They lived on the Quay Clovelly and Charles was a fisherman. Arthur was one of seven, and his siblings were (Arthur), Alice, Fred, Charlie, Nellie, Percy, and Jack. Arthur went to Clovelly School and his school master was John Zelden. When he left school he got a job at Hartland Abbey and then went to work with Major General Lord Cheylesmore from Kensington in London as a valet (gentleman's dresser). When war broke out, Lord Cheylesmore wanted Arthur to go to London with him to join up and be a bugle boy for him. But Arthur decided not to and he returned home to join his local Devonshire regiment. He enlisted in Bideford and went onto Exeter when they first called for volunteers. He joined with his friends Samuel Oke and Monty Jeffery. Arthur junior remembers his father saying 'When he went to enlist there were thousands of us, gentry, ordinary working people and vagabonds and when we were all stripped down and bathed you couldn't tell one from the other'. He completed his training as a soldier near Salisbury.

They were all put on board a ship at Southampton locked in the holds and sailed to France and were billeted into camp. A few days later they marched to the front lines and dug trenches and after they had been there a few days they started to see dead bodies and body parts, which was a great shock to them as they had never seen anything like that before; it was soon to become normal life for them all. They stayed on the front line for about 11 days at a time. With weeks of continual rain, Arthur witnessed men and horses lost in the mud. Arthur junior recalls his father talking about how tired and hungry they were and that they would fall asleep with gun in hand and wake up and just keep shooting, although they did not know what they were shooting at. Arthur kept a daily diary and map of his movements in France. All the soldiers liked the foreign currency which worked in 10s.

Arthur had some medical experience and when the 75th Field Ambulance was formed due to the heavy losses they were taking, he put himself forward. With the Field Ambulance he served on Vimy Ridge, Passchendaele, Messines Ridge and the Somme. It is remarkable that he survived this service on or close to the front lines.

A Field Ambulance team including Arthur crossed no mans land in an advance. They were following British soldiers. There was a large shell explosion leaving a deep crater which Arthur and his fellow medical corps went into. Arthur treated some British wounded including a soldier whose abdomen was hanging out, Arthur folded his injured abdomen back into his body and bound him up as best he could. As the Field Ambulance team (like the one pictured on the next page) were treating the wounded the Germans advanced and were looking down on the British in the crater from the top. The Germans took Arthur and the rest of the men (but not the wounded) as prisoners of war and they declared that they will leave the British wounded and will now be treating and carrying the German wounded back behind the German lines. The families of these men were sent home telegrams saying 'missing presumed dead'. They worked behind the German lines for several days and then were moved to a farmhouse which was housing prisoners of war. Arthur remembers his father talking about how the Germans feared the fierce Scots. In the farmhouse there were a lot of Scottish prisoners of war, and they burnt down three big

farmhouses, and the Germans were fearful of the 'Women from Hell'. Arthur junior remembers Arthur talking about their time as prisoners of war when the Germans could not get any food in due to a British blockade at sea. The Germans and the prisoners of war were starving and eating any raw peelings they could get hold of and living off the land and hedges.

Just before the war ended they were released, although no one was to know in case the enemy found out. When he returned home and knocked on his parents' door, his father answered and nearly had a heart attack; they had accepted that he was dead. Arthur then returned to do two more years of service after the war had finished. He was sent to Palestine and later Egypt where he worked in pathology labs doing experiments on diseases.

In the sixties Arthur lived in 32 North Hill, Clovelly and his son Arthur was now a teenager. One day there was a knock at the door and it was a man and his wife. Arthur's wife answered the door and the man said 'I'm looking for Arthur Shackson'. She went to get him and when he saw Arthur he said 'I've got the right man, I can see by your blue eyes, you won't remember me but you jumped into a shell crater ...' and Arthur said 'you're not the soldier whose abdomen was hanging out?' and he replied 'yes I am'. The soldier had survived and once he had recovered worked in an office dealing with military awards. He asked to see Arthur's award, which Arthur knew nothing about, but the soldier swore that Arthur should have received an award for his bravery for volunteering to go into the crater.

66049 Pte Arthur Shackson.
c/8 Field Amb.
R. A. M. C

BUCKINGHAM PALACE

1918.

The Queen joins me in welcoming
you on your release from the
miseries & hardships, which you have
endured with so much patience &
courage.

During these many months of trial,
the early rescue of our gallant Officers
& Men from the cruelties of their captivity
has been uppermost in our thoughts.

We are thankful that this longed
for day has arrived, & that back in
the old Country you will be able
once more to enjoy the happiness of
a home & to see good days among
those who anxiously look for your
return.

George R.I.

Serial No. *13317 Rawe*   Army Form B. 2079.

NOTE—This Certificate is to be issued without any altera-tions in the manuscript.

Certificate of discharge of No. *66019* Rank *Private*

Name... *SHACKSON*   *ARTHUR*
        Surname.   Christian Names in full.

Unit*
and   } *R. A. M. Corps*
Regiment or Corps
from which discharged
*The unit of the Regiment or Corps such as Field Co. R.E., H.T. or M.T., A.S.C., etc., is invariably to be stated.

Regiment or Corps to which first posted. *3rd Devon Regt*

Also previously served in...

....

....

Only Regiments or Corps in which the soldier served since August 4th, 1914, are to be stated. If inapplicable this space is to be ruled through in ink and initialled.

Specialist Qualifications (Military)... *Nil*

Medals, Clasps,   { * *Nil*   *Church of England Nil*
Decorations and   *Nil*   Wound Stripes* *Nil*
Mentions in dispatches   *Nil*   To be inserted in words.

Has served Overseas on Active Service†

Enlisted at *Bideford* on *22 — 5* — 191*5*
        * Each space is to be filled in and the word "nil" inserted where necessary.
        †To be struck out in ink if not applicable.

He is discharged in consequence of *Re-enlistment under*
H. O. 4 of 1919. ....

....

after serving* *Three* years* *988* days with the Colours, and
................years* ....days in the *Army Reserve* } Strike out
                                                        or { whichever
                                        Territorial Force† } inapplicable
* Each space is to be filled in and the word "nil" inserted where necessary; number of years to be written in words.
†Service with Territorial Force to be shown only in cases of soldiers serving on a T.F. attestation.

Date of discharge. *24 — 7 — 19*

.... *Lt Col* } Signature
                                              and
                                              Rank.
        Officer i/c *R A M C* Records.
        Woking. ....(Place).

Description of the above-named soldier when he left the Colours.

Year of Birth... *1895*   Marks or Scars.................

Height... *5* ft *3* in. ....

Complexion.................................

Eyes............ Hair.................

(A11039) Wt.W1912 PP1138. 240,000 6/18. **Sch. 44.** D.D.& L.   [P.T.O.

Vimy Ridge & Mt Saint Eloi

May 22/1916

The Vally of the Dead

While sitting at my dugout door
A frenchman passed me by
To get in conversation
I though I have a try
I asked him What they named the place
He quickly turned & said
In rather broken English
Its the Valley of the Dead

2

I asked him what his meaning was
And How they ever came
to give that quiet Valley such a wearied
(gruesome name)
Then he talked of last September
When the frenchmen fought & Bled
& lost that 14 thousand in the Vally
(of the Dead

<u>**Poem by Arthur Shackson**</u>
Vimy Ridge and Mount Saint Eloi
May 22nd 1916
The Valley of the Dead

While sitting in my dugout door
a Frenchman passed me by
To get in conversation I thought Id have a try
I asked him what they named this place
He quickly turned and said
In rather broken English its the Valley of the Dead

I asked him what his meaning was
and how they ever came
to give that quiet valley such a weird and gruesome name
Then he talked of last September
when the Frenchmen fought and bled
and lost that 17 thousand in the Valley of the Dead.

Said he the Frenchman charge that day
as Frenchmen always will
they got the Germans on the run
and chased them up the hill
then down into the valley
by their brave Commander led
they massacred 2 army corps
in the Valley of the Dead

Said he if you don't believe me
just walk 50 yards away and you will
find there verification for every word I say
It was there in last September
when the grass with blood was red
the French men charged the Germans
in the Valley of the Dead

I walked across a sight I saw
I never shall forget men who had
fallen 6 months ago had not been buried yet
Some sights you see are soon forgotten
but this one turned my head
that awful gruesome spectacle
in the Valley of the Dead.

Pte A Shackson no 66019
75 F.A. R.A.M.C. B.E.F.

Just before the battle mother I am thinking dear of you.

<u>Letter from the King</u>
Buckingham Palace
1918

The Queen joins me in welcoming you on your release from the miseries and hardships, which you have endured with so much patience and courage.

During these many months of trial, the early rescue of our gallant officers and men from the cruelties of their captivity has been uppermost in our thoughts.

We are thankful that this longed for day has arrived, and that back in the old Country you will be able once more to enjoy the happiness of a home and to see good days among those who anxiously look for your return.

George R.J.

The War Diary of Leonard Lott

Many of the combatants of the First World War recorded the daily events of their experiences in the form of a diary. This was strictly illegal because they could carry information that might eventually fall into enemy hands. Some were subsequently published after the war and have become celebrated. Many more, however, remained tucked away in a cupboard or drawers for years, unpublished and unseen. The world wide web has given an opportunity for the descendants of many survivors to publish fragments of diary entries for the education and interest of others.

The brief diary of Leonard Lott is one of these and this chapter is devoted to his war diary. We are indebted to Gordon and Ted Lott for allowing us to use his words and for the brief biography recorded later in this chapter.

"Leonard James Lott was born at Ford in Alwington on September 5th 1898 and after leaving school worked on the family farm. The family built up milk production, on their farm, supplying a dairy in Bideford and eventually starting their own round.

Leonard was originally called up when conscription was introduced and due to the nature of the family business applied for exemption which was granted. The military appealed this decision and a tribunal examined his case. It was reported that his family business was run on a farm of 139 acres at Fairy Cross. The military stated that the farm was well served with labour having his father, two men one a horseman aged 28 and the other a cattleman aged 23 who had already been granted exemption, as well as his mother and two sisters. This case was characterised as one of the clearest ones when a man should not be exempted. Mr. Metherell who represented many agricultural workers as their advocate stated that Leonard was needed on the farm due to his father's ill health and he went on to explain that many poorer customers could not afford meat so the cream that he supplied was not a luxury but a necessity of life. On January 1st the military were deemed to have won and Leonard was to be enlisted. He had only reached the age for conscription the previous September so the enlistment officers must have been on his case extremely quickly given that he had already been exempted once between those dates.

He announced, to family members, that he had been asked too many times why he was not in uniform and signed up in Bideford a few days later.

His diary describes his training and experiences he had in France, he did not speak much about the war and only told Gordon one or two of them. Once when charging across no mans land he dived into a foxhole only to land on top of a German soldier who he reckoned had been dead for a fortnight. Another time their group had been pinned down by a machine gun battery and a junior officer asked his superior officer for permission to take a volunteer and destroy the post in the night. Private Lott and the officer crept up to the machine gun later and he said that he could hear the Germans talking, he did not say what happened next but as it states in his diary that he was a grenadier, later to be called bombers, who threw grenades, so one could only guess at the outcome.

After the war he came home and, in his early twenties, he married Ada Wood in 1922 and took on the farm at Ford running a successful producer retailer milk round, winning prizes for clean milk production, some pupils from Woolsery School visited his farm to study his methods. There were no children born of the marriage.

He had the reputation of being a crack shot with the twelve bore gun and different people have reported that they used to tell him he should go and have a cigarette or something so that they would have a chance to get the gun to their shoulder and get a shot at a rabbit or pheasant.

A memory Gordon had of him was his gift of telling a good yarn and his laughter afterwards, I recall he had retired and was helping with our corn harvest, having our tea in the field sitting by some sheaves, he told a yarn started laughing and was rolling on the ground trying to get his breath back. He loved his lawn bowls and his bell ringing in later life. He passed away in July 1976".

We are grateful to Gordon Lott for this information.

Excerpts from his diaries

Private Leonard James Lott of the 5th Battalion Worcester regiment kept a small cash book as a diary and the entries were written with a pencil. Some of his entries were written on the battlefield so were particularly difficult to write and unfortunately some words have faded or become obscured.

I have some letters written by soldiers in the Boer War some sixteen or seventeen years earlier to my great grandfather, also in pencil, almost certainly the indelible type and it is amazing how they have stood the test of time. Lazlo Biro was still a young man and had not yet created his invention and a fountain pen would have been totally impractical so a pencil was the only option. He also used it to record the addresses of presumably some of his comrades in arms. He was not a Woolsery man but is closely related to a well known local family of long standing and his experiences must have been very similar to those of our village heroes.

Some of the place names he mentioned have been impossible to identify from his words but understandably a teenaged soldier in a foreign land would have written down what he heard, no doubt all signposts etc. had long since been obliterated to confound the enemy by which ever side was in occupation. His diary is unsurprisingly written in note form rather than flowing prose and no doubt if he could have been persuaded to sit down in later life to record his experiences an even more fascinating tale would have unfolded. It still can make one's blood run cold to think you are reading words written in a shell hole being bombarded by the enemy.

In the following script I have copied his writings verbatim but the italicised script are my explanations etc.

His initial training took place at Horton Camp in the Devizes area early in 1917 where his expert experience with a twelve bore stood him in good stead and he was presented with first prize by Lieutenant Colonel Chatterley for being the best shot in his platoon and it may have been this which caused him to be made temporary leader of his group, a position usually given to a sergeant or possibly a corporal, whilst he was still a private. Len's equipment, that he lists, were 1 waist belt, 1 pair of braces, 1 haversack, one entrenching tool and carrier with handle and straps, 2 pouches, 1 water bottle and carrier, 1 mess tin and cover, 1 rifle number 156729, 1 bayonet, 1 oil bottle and pull through.

Under clothing of a soldier he is list includes 2 pairs of Ankle boots and one pair ...., 1 service dress cap, 1 mug, 2 service drawers, 1 swagger cane, 1 great coat, 2 service dress jackets, 1 pair pattes, 2 pairs trousers, 1 sweater, 1 pr braces, button hook, 1 brushes, 1 cap com. 1 comb, 1 fork, 1 holster belt, 1 house wife*(a sewing kit)*, 1 knife, 3 shirts, 3 pairs of socks,1 spoon, 1 pair shoulder ......tin of polish, cap badge 1 razor, apiece of soap, 2 towels. *In the British Army prior to World War I swagger sticks were carried by all other ranks when off duty, as part of their walking out uniform. The stick took the* *form of a short cane of polished wood, with an ornamented metal head of regimental pattern. The usual custom was for the private soldier or NCO to carry the stick tucked under his arm. You probably thought as I did that the swagger stick was an appendage merely for the officer classes not the rank and file. This was the case in later years but not at that time.*

He left Horton Camp on April 2nd for France and landed at Le Havre on the 4th then proceeded to Rouen and from there to Aire hospital with a mouth infection. The Germans bombed the town and did extensive damage with 50 killed and injured.

Left Horton camp (Devizes area, Wiltshire) April 12th en route for France. Landed Le Havre

4th Proceeded by boat to Rouen to Cyclists base depot. *A base depot was a holding camp. Situated within easy distance of one the Channel ports, it received men on arrival from England and kept them in training while they awaiting posting to a unit at the front. It was inland so presumably they travelled up the River Seine to Rouen* Arrived 5th and sent to Aire

May 1st to the village of Crelquelles under training at 5th Army Corps .

On 15th May I was admitted into 54th CCS Hospital , impetigo on face and transferred on

17th to 39th CCS HospitaL at Aire with poisoned face. Germans bombed town on the nights of 17th 18th 19th and 20th and did extensive damage.

On the 19th over 50 killed and injured also shelled railway yard but no damage done. June 3rd sent to Battalion (Mullingham) *possibly Mazinghem* transport lines 4th Proceeded to Gaurbesque near Buriguett. *This is a few miles from Boulogne so Leonard had been sent quite a few miles north to re join the war effort.*

On June 28th went into action in front of Trippe Farm, Le Bassee Sector.

*The main **Battle of La Bassée** was fought by German and Franco-British forces in northern France in October 1914, during reciprocal attempts by the opposing armies to envelop the northern flank of their opponent, which has been called the Race to the Sea. The German 6th Army took Lille before a British force could secure the town and the 4th Army attacked the exposed British flank at Ypres. The British were driven back and the German Army occupied La Bassée and Neuve Chapelle. Around 15 October, the British recaptured Givenchy-lès-la-Bassée but failed to recover La Bassée. German reinforcements arrived and regained the initiative, until the arrival of the Lahore Division of the Indian Corps. The British repulsed German attacks until early November, after which both sides concentrated their resources on the First Battle of Ypres and the battle at La Bassée was reduced to local operations. In late January and early February 1915, German and British troops conducted raids and local attacks in the Affairs of Cuinchy, which took place at Givenchy-lès-la-Bassée and just south of La Bassée Canal, leaving the front line little changed. This situation was still ongoing when Leonard arrived almost three years later.*

Relieved on 6th July. Shelled heavily on coming out eventually landed at La Macquilerie

15th proceeded down line to Quermes

22nd July, Marched to Lansys Aug 6th Nieppe forest. Again in action.2nd Warwicks went over assisted by 2/6

Entered enemy lines, on morning of 7inst. We advanced 2 miles to Meone , our little home a shell hole, in which I am entering this.

9th over the top, left of right sector 4 section first to enter Merville, found bridges blown up.

On 10th shot down enemy? Shield and Harris were killed on going out to it.

Unable to find a record of the burial of either men.

12th August relieved by Worcesters and went back to forest for a rest.

The next page of his diary itemises a list of presumably new equipment he received it included: 2 button sticks, 1 button brush, 2 blacking, 3 soldiers friend, 2 toothbrush, soap. *A soldier's friend was a tin containing a portable candle holder. Autumn was approaching so this would have been a requirement particularly if your water was frozen.*

He then lists R Grenadier Section

- Cpl Lubbock
- Ben Jordan
- Len Lott
- Percy Hilling
- W.Russ

A *grenadier (from French, derived from the word grenade) was originally a specialized soldier, first established as a distinct role in the mid-to-late 17th century, for the throwing of grenades and sometimes assault operations. At that time grenadiers were chosen from the strongest and largest soldiers.*

August 22nd Again in action Germans now begin their retirement. We advance about 5 miles . capture town of St Estaires, dig in and again push forward. Held up by machine gun fire and narrowly missed Blightly however we lie in a ditch for 5 hrs and save our Bacon.

Sept1st our platoon begins its Gallant bit of work, The grenadiers assisted by Lewis gunners attack enemy strongpoint in behind, here we drove him, taking 15 prisoners a … major holding his position his artillery retaliated giving us a bumping with 5/qs and sending over about 2000. Sam Dyer, Reg Foster, Hopkins and J Kneale fell a shell killing 3 and reg killed by a whizz bang 2 yards away from me. *A light shell fired from one of the smaller calibre field guns, referring to the sound as the shell came to explode.*

We buried them in Anzac cemetery and then were relieved for a well earned rest where we made bivouac near to Luille Le lac. Entrained later for Doulon marched to Havrincourt in front of Cambria near to Bourlon Wood.

At dawn Monday Oct 26th over the top a terrible fight 5 divisions, *several thousand men,* taking part. We attacked a village which was indeed a veritable fortress with machine guns and we captured 100 guns, 4 trench mortars 2 field guns and thousands of prisoners. We suffered heavy casualties in this. Fritz had dammed up the canal which we – Percy, Russ, Oliver and Riley were all killed my firm pals.

George Varrilow and Pitts wounded.
On 28th we were relieved by 24th Devons who advanced after a hard battle captured Valenciennes with 4000 prisoners.

Oct 29th Admitted to hospital with shrapnel wounds and influenza sent to Cambria then to Bapaune

Oct 31st went to Red X where I am in 26 General Hospital

This is the last entry in his little cash book his war was happily short, he was not legally old enough to serve until September 1916 when he celebrated his eighteenth birthday and he must have arrived back on the family farm some time soon after the twentieth anniversary of his birth.

Ian Adams remembers his great uncle who died in WW1 and also his grandfather who fought in WW1.

Fredrick John Benjamin Webzell was Ian's great uncle and Ian has collected information about his service after finding a box of birth certificates and medals in his father's briefcase. Fredrick was born in 1889 and was 26 years old when he enlisted on 29th December 1915 in Woolwich. He served in the Royal Horse Artillery and Royal Field Artillery as 68291 Saddler and served in the 37th Siege Battery. Fredrick was reported in despatches as serving with the Expeditionary Forces in France and also served in Egypt. Fredrick died on the 4th August 1916 of wounds received in action. The family where told that he was wounded by machine gun fire across his abdomen and after receiving these injuries he

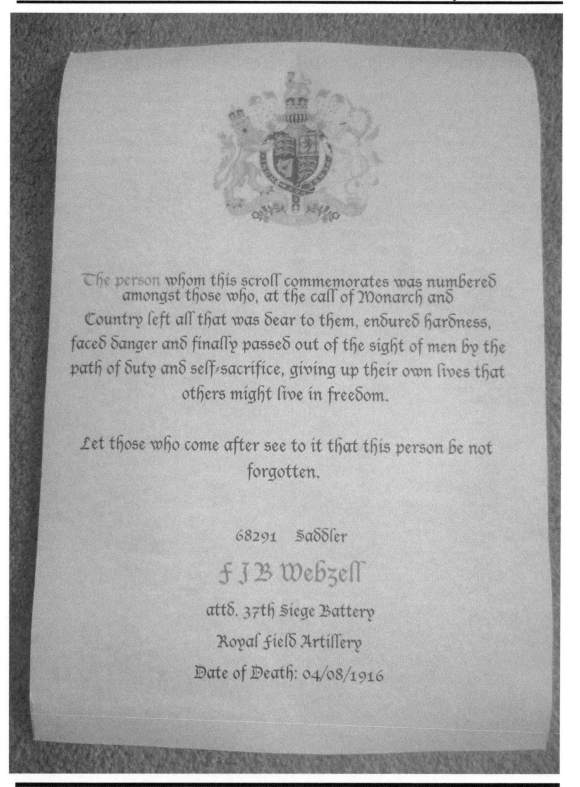

The person whom this scroll commemorates was numbered amongst those who, at the call of Monarch and Country left all that was dear to them, endured hardness, faced danger and finally passed out of the sight of men by the path of duty and self-sacrifice, giving up their own lives that others might live in freedom.

Let those who come after see to it that this person be not forgotten.

68291   Saddler

F J B Webzell

attd. 37th Siege Battery

Royal Field Artillery

Date of Death: 04/08/1916

carried a wounded colleague back to the nursing station where his colleague survived and Fredrick then passed away. He left a wife and two children. Fredrick is buried in France Heilly Station Cemetery Mericourt L`Abbe. He received the Victory Medal, British War Medal, 1915 Star, and of course the death penny and scroll. Ian has a replica scroll and the wording is:

The person who this scroll commemorates was numbered amongst those who at the call of the monarch and country left all that was dear to them, endured hardness, faced danger and finally passed out of the sight of men, by the path of duty and self sacrifice, giving up their own lives that other might live in freedom.

Let those who come after see to it that this person be not forgotten.

68291 Saddler
F.J.B. Webzell
Attd. 37th Siege Battery
Royal Field Artillery
Date of Death: 04.08.16

Charles Albert Webzell used the name Chas and signed up with his brother Fredrick in Woolwich in December 1915. He was in the Merchant Navy serving as a stoker. He was 12744 Saddler in the Middlesex Regiment 2nd Battalion and 3rd Royal Sussex Regiment of the Royal Field Artillery. He served in France where he received shrapnel injuries and was discharged from the Army on 20th August 1918. It was later on in January 1946 where he finally succumbed to his wounds. On returning from the Army he was a stoker in the local paper mill. He was married in 1912 before he went to war and had his first child in 1914 and then on return had a daughter Grace Ellen Mary (Ian Adams mother) who was born 1916. Charles receive the British War Medal, which Ian has, and the Victory Medal which went to Ian's cousin.

The Snape family and the Victoria Cross

James Miller was the uncle of my grandfather James Arnold, and therefore the great-great-great-uncle of my son Keiran Snape.

James Miller was born on 13th March 1890 at Taylor's Farm, Houghton near Preston, the son of George and Mary Miller. The family later moved to 1 Ollerton Terrace, Withnell, near Chorley and James worked in the local paper mill at Withnell Fold. Miller enlisted on the outbreak of war. As No. 12639 Private James Miller, he joined one of Lord Kitchener's New Army Units, the 7th Battalion King's Own Royal Lancaster Regiment, which was raised at Bowerham Barracks in September 1914.

Miller went overseas with 7th Battalion King's Own in July 1915. He saw action at Lens and Loos in the autumn, before to moving to the Somme in April 1916.

The Battalion was in action at La Boiselle between 3rd-7th July and spent the end of July consolidating a position near Mametz Wood and Bazentin-le-Petit.

After the battalion captured enemy positions near Bazentin-le-Petit, on 30th July. Miller was ordered to take a message across the lines during a break in communications. The *London Gazette* recorded his act of gallantry:-

"For most conspicuous bravery. His battalion was consolidating a position after its capture by assault. Private Miller was ordered to take an important message under heavy shell and rifle fire, and to bring back a reply at all costs. He was compelled to cross the open, and on leaving the trench was shot almost immediately in the back, the bullet coming through his abdomen. In spite of this, with heroic courage and self-sacrifice, he compressed the gaping wound in his abdomen, delivered his message, staggered back with his answer, and fell dead at the feet of the officer to whom he delivered it. He gave his life with a supreme devotion to duty. "

James Miller is buried in Dartmoor Cemetery near Becordel on the Somme. A Celtic Cross of Cornish granite was erected on the edge of Withnell village churchyard. This memorial was paid for by public subscription. It was cleaned and restored in 1988. The Victoria Cross was presented to Miller's father by King George V at Buckingham Palace. Ellis

Williams, a former Colour Sergeant ^ in the King's Own and the then Secretary of the Old Comrades Association, recorded Miller's gallantry in a contemporary poem entitled " The Message"

Now, put away your books, my lads; come sit you by my side;
And I'll tell you the glorious story how Miller, of Withnell died.
I've told you oft of the Spartan boy, how Spartans nobly bore
Themselves to guard the narrow pass, in the grand old days of yore.
You have read great Nelson's story, of Trafalgar, 'cross the foam;
And also of the dauntless three who held the bridge at Rome.
I've told you, too, of Gordon's death, the bravest of the brave,
And of the noble Kitchener, now gone to his ocean grave;
But none fell nobler than this lad, of Lancashire the pride,
So let your children's children tell how Jimmy Miller died.

K.C. 272 e   NEG 468   KO 272/95

To the Glorious Memory of
PRIVATE JAMES MILLER, V.C.,
Late of the King's Own Royal
Lancaster Regiment,

Died of wounds in France, July 30th, 1916.

Aged 26 years.

The Story of the Message.

By ELLIS WILLIAMS

(Hon. Sec., The King's Own Old Comrades'
Association).

We had shelled the Hun from his dug-outs, our batteries had smashed him in style,
We had hurled the foe from his trenches, driven him back for a mile:
But many a hero had fallen, many a husband and son,
Who'd gone to their rest, left us weakened. Could we hold that which we had won?
So our captain cried out, "Here, Miller! A message to Company D.
I know you and trust you well, Miller, so bring back the answer to me.
You never have yet shirked a duty, you never have reasoned why;
For God's sake do not fail me now, but bring me the reply.

I hate to ask this sacrifice, but it's the only way,
If you but get this message through you'll save some lives to-day."

Just a brief salute to his officer; he cleared the trench at a bound.
He dashed out into the open, out on the shell swept ground,
With a hearty cheer from his comrades. The rest is hard to tell,
But, with scarce a score of paces gone, and angry bullet fell
And pierced him through from back to side. He halted for a span
(Ye shot not well, O marksman, to slay so brave a man!),
Then pressed his hand firm on his wound and gamely struggled on.

So got his message through at last, his short life all but gone.
"Now stay you here, brave Miller, you have nobly run your race;
And you are sorely wounded, lad. Let another take your place."
"Don't ask it, sir. Why waste a life? You're open to attack.

I've brought this message right through hell -
I'll take the answer back."
Then brave men sobbed as he started off across that danger zone.
They could not, dare not, "queer his pitch"; that's a creed in the old King's Own.
So he reels along in his agony, now on his knees he crawls,
With his life's blood ebbing drop by drop; a dozen stumbles and falls.
But the goal is reached as he murmurs, "Relief - sir - all - is - well."
Then he dropped at his captain's feet and died.
So Miller of Withnell fell.

His name is off the roll call now; so brave where all were brave.
He's laid by gallant soldiers in his lonely honoured grave.
He saw his duty plain and straight, he went for it there and then,
So I think our Saviour won't be hard on a man that died for men.
Cheer up, ye hearts of England! Cheer up, ye Britons all!
Bear up, ye wives and mothers, so sick at duty's call.
The soul of our race is in men like these, who fight till latest breath,
And, like the sentinel of old, stand "faithful unto death!"
This deed yet stands aloof from all, heroic, grand, alone;
The pride of all the British race, the pride of the old King's Own.
So when you hear folk talk of heroes tell this story far and wide,
This story of "The Message: How Miller of Withnell died."

Jonathan Downes remembers his grandfather

Both my grandfathers fought in the Great War, although my paternal grandfather eventually died of his wounds gained in Gallipoli, a few years before I was born. My mother's father, however, was a fighter pilot in the Royal Flying Corps and he didn't die until 1972 so I knew him, although - as I spent most of my childhood in Hong Kong - not as well as I would have liked.

In 1971 my family returned to England, and for several months we stayed in a village near to where Gran and Grandad lived in Hampshire in a house called *Mole End* named after the burrow 'Moley' lived in, in *Wind in the Willows*. I would like to say that this was the time in my life when I got to know my grandparents. But that would be a lie, and – except when I tell great big steaming lies for comic effect – I always try to tell the truth in my writing. Although I was superficially close to my grandmother, my memories of her are fairly ambivalent. Indeed, when she came to live with us in North Devon in 1974, after my grandfather's death, it was not a happy time. I do, however, remember one particularly intense episode when I got to know my grandfather quite well. Poor old chap. He was born on August 8th 1888 (all the 8s as he proudly used to proclaim) and was 83 by the time we arrived back in England. My father disliked him, and my mother and grandfather basically treated him – with gentle good humour – as an irrelevance. He had once been an excellent carpenter and had built *Mole End* and most of its furniture. But now, in his twilight years, he was content to sit in the corner of his sitting room, puffing away on an evil-smelling old pipe, and dreaming what was left of his life away.

Lest We Forget

However, one day, he took me for a walk. Taking me firmly by the hand he marched down the garden, past the garage to the front gate, and we walked onto the road outside. Opposite *Mole End* was a field gate, and in the field was a crop of ripening barley, interspersed with bright red poppies. *"Go over and pick one of those red flowers"* my grandfather instructed me, and I trotted over to do his bidding. I still can vividly remember the peculiar paper-like texture of the petals, which seemed so much at odds with the sturdy stalk and flowerhead. I brought it back to the old man, who stood erect; every inch the old soldier. There were tears rolling down his cheeks. I didn't know what to do. Big boys don't cry, and at 83 he was certainly too old to be blubbing. *"Each of those poppies is a friend of mine"* he said. *"...and each one is like that poor bastard"* he coughed, gesturing to a dead crow that had been shot by a farmer and then hung, as if crucified, on a barbed wire fence *pour encourager les autres*. He stood for a moment, then turned on his heel and marched back into the house. It is the only time I ever remember seeing him leave *Mole End*, and one of the only times I ever saw him not sitting, puffing away on his evil-smelling old briar pipe, with a checkered red and brown blanket over his knees.

I hardly knew him. It has been well over forty years since he died, and I am a grandfather now myself. But whenever I hear *The Green Fields of France* I think of him and cry a little bit inside so that nobody can see.

APPENDIX: Clovelly in the Great War

An excerpt from the North Devon Journal 8th April 1920.

Barely has the church of All Saints been so crowded as on Sunday morning on the occasion of the unveiling and dedication of the brass memorial tablet, erected to the everlasting memory of Clovelly men who laid down their lives in the recent war. The tablet which has been erected by the relatives and friends of the fallen heroes consists of a repotisse brass tablet, two feet by eighteen inches, mounted on polished black slate. The centre of the tablet is occupied by a strikingly beautiful representation of St. George and the Dragon. At the top are two crossed swords with the Cross of our saviour, and the appropriate words "Fight the good fight". The inscription on the tablet reads "To the honoured memory of the Clovelly men who gave their lives in the Great war 1914-1918. " On each side of the central figure are the names, in alphabetical order, of the men who made the great sacrifice :-

William P. Babb

Job Beer

James Bond

Charles Callaghan

Samuel P. Colwill

George Cook

James T. Cruse

Thomas W. Cruse

Stanley B. Headon

William T. Howard

Clovelly Church

Harry Jewell
Llewellyn R. Pengilly
Thomas S. Pengilly
James H. Somerville,
William Stevens
Frank Tardivel
William A.B. Tuke

At Sunday's service which was of a very impressive nature, the Rev T.l.V. Simkin (Rector) officiated the brass being unveiled by Mrs Hamlyn. A special form of service was used, the memorial hymn " O valiant hearts etc" being sung with deep feeling. The rector's sermon which was delivered with great emotion was based on the text "They loved not their lives into the death." The memorial brass was designed by Messrs F. Osborne and Co. of London

Clovelly War Memorial

Information from Devon Heritage and CWGC websites compiled by Jane Cann

C1	W.P.BABB	20764 Private William P. Babb of the 8th Battalion, the Devonshire Regiment. Born in Clovelly in 1891, Son of William P. and Mary Ann Babb of Burscott, Clovelly, Devon. Died 4 October 1917 aged 27. Remembered with Honour at the Tyne Cot Memorial, West-Vlaanderen Belgium where 34948 casualties are remembered.
C2	J.BEER	B/201888 Private Job Beer of the 1st/28th Battalion, the London Regiment (The Artist's Rifles). Born in Woolsery in 1886. Husband of Sarah Beer of 136 Dyke Green Clovelly North Devon. Died 29th March 1918 aged 32. Remembered with Honour at Doullens Communal Cemetery Extension No.2, Somme France where 375 casualties are remembered.
C3	J.BOND	53474 Private James Bond of the Royal Army Medical Corps. Born in Hartland in 1894. Son of John and Emma Bond. Died 28th July 1915. Remembered with Honour at All Saints Churchyard, Clovelly.
C4	C.CALLAGHAN	45400 Sergeant Charles Callaghan 'D' Battery 256th Brigade. Royal Field Artillery and Royal Horse Artillery. Son of Mrs J. Callaghan, of Park Side House, Maple Street, Huddersfield and the late inspector Callaghan of Huddersfield Police force. He died 30th December 1917 aged 30. He was awarded the Military Medal. Remembered with Honour at Huddersfield (Edgerton) Cemetery.
C5	S.P.COLWILL	15721 Private Samuel P. Colwill of the 1st Battalion, the Devonshire Regiment. Son of Daniel and Elizabeth Colwill of Stoke, Hartland. Born in Hartland in 1889. Died 6 November 1917 aged 28. Remembered with Honour at Tyne Cot Memorial, West-Vlaanderen Belgium where 34948 casualties are remembered.
C6	G.COOK	20815 Private George Cook of the 9th Battalion, the Devonshire Regiment. He was born in Hartland in 1890 and lived in Clovelly. Son of Thomas and Fanny Cook of Lower Dyke, Clovelly. Died 13 July 1916 aged 26. Remembered with Honour at All Saints Church Yard Clovelly.
C7	J.T.CRUSE	Able Seaman and Lamps, James Thomas. Cruse of the Mercantile Marine *SS Kilmaho* of Cardiff. Born in Clovelly in 1885. Son of Thomas and Catherine Tucker Cruse of 75 High Street Clovelly; husband of Caroline Cruse of 25 High Street Clovelly; brother of Thomas (see below). Died 17 May 1917 aged 32. Remembered with Honour at Tower Hill Memorial, London where 35767 casualties are remembered.
C8	T.W.CRUSE	Able Seaman Thomas William Cruse of the Mercantile Marine *SS Kilmaho* of Cardiff. Son of Thomas and Catherine Tucker Cruse of 75 High Street Clovelly; brother of James Cruse (See above) Born in Clovelly in 1891. Died 17 May 1917 aged 27. Remembered with Honour at Tower Hill Memorial, London where 35767 casualties are remembered.

C9	S.B.HEADON	12/1416 Private Stanley Braund Headon of the Kings Own Light Infantry. Son of Minnie and the late Josiah. Born in Bucks Mills in the September Quarter of 1900. Discharged from the army as under age. After (unsuccessfully) trying to join the Navy, he joined the Mercantile Marine and served as a steward on board SS *Kepwick Hall*. He died when that ship sank off the United States 7 November 1918, aged 18.
C10	W.T.HOWARD	11478 Acting Corporal, the Devonshire Regiment. Son of Thomas and Hannah Howard; husband of Martha Howard. Born in Bittadon in the September Quarter of 1868. Died 1 July 1916 aged 48.
C11	H.JEWELL	102725 Private Harry Jewell of the 4th Battalion, the Machine Gun Infantry Corps. Born in 1899. Son of Mrs Mary Jane Jewell of 106 High Street Clovelly. Lived in Bideford. Died 24 April 1918 aged 19. Remembered with Honour at Loos Memorial
C12	L.R.PENGILLY	37600 Air Mechanic 1st Class Llewellyn Richard Pengilly of the RAF. Son of Richard and Grace Pengilly of Clovelly; husband of Margaret Annie Bradford (formerly Pengilly) of HM Coastguard Station, Stoke Hartland. Born in Clovelly in 1886. Died 31 October aged 33. Remembered with Honour at All Saints Churchyard Clovelly.
C13	T.S.PENGILLY	Able Seaman Thomas Stanbury. Pengilly of the Mercantile Marine, SS *Kilmalio (Cardiff)*. Born in Clovelly in 1877. Son of Richard and Grace Pengilly; husband of Edith Pengilly (nee Pennington) of 44 Clovelly; brother of Llewellyn (see above). Died 17 May 1917 aged 40. Remembered with Honour at Rhiw (St Aelrhiw) Churchyard, Caernarvonshire Wales.
C14	J.H.SOMERVILLE	19867 Driver James H. Somerville of the 8th Brigade, the Australian Field Artillery. Son of James and Augusta Somerville of Clovelly. Born in 1893. Died 2 July 1916 aged 23, he died of heart failure (BB).
C15	W.STEVENS	4516 Lance Corporal William Stevens of the 109th Coy, the Machine Gun Infantry Corps. Born in 1893. Son of William Stevens of Burscott and the late Augusta (or Angelina) Stevens of Clovelly. Died 16 August 1917 aged 24. Remembered with Honour at the Tyne Cot Memorial, West-Vlaanderen Belgium where 34948 casualties are remembered.
C16	F.TARDIVEL	279894 Petty Officer Stoker Frank (François) Tardivel RNVR formerly of the Coast Guard, serving on *HMS Laurentic*. Son of François and Ann Marie Tardivel. Born in St Peters, Jersey, CI on 16 June 1876. Died 25 January 1917 aged 41 when the Laurentic was lost. Buried in St Mura's Churchyard, Upper Fahan Ireland.
C17	W.A.B.TUKE	6384 Sergt. William Abraham Brenchley Tuke of the 2nd/4th City of Bristol Battalion, the Gloucestershire Regiment. Son of Harry and Eliza Tuke of The Gardens, Clovelly Court, Born in October 1894. Died 19 July 1916 in the UK aged 21. Remembered with Honour at Rue-Du-Bois Military Cemetery, Fleurbaix Pas de Calais France where 450 casualties are remembered.
C18	James Henry Shackson	Born Clovelly. PTE 201294 of the 1st/4th Battalion Norfolk Regiment. Died 19th April 1917 in Palestine. Remembered on the Jerusalem Memorial, Israel and Palestine (including Gaza) where 3301 men are remembered.

The following men are not names on the Clovelly memorial but died at war and have a link to Clovelly, thank you to Brian Barrows for these names.

C19	James Bate	PTE 2567 James Bate of the 1st/4th Battalion Devonshire Regiment. Born Clovelly. Son of Thomas and Susan Bate, of 84 Clovelly. Died 3rd Feb 1917 aged 25. He is buried in Amara War Cemetery where 3696 casualties are remembered. He enlisted in Axminster and died in Iraq(BB).
C20	William Bickle	PTE 21776 William Bickle of 12th Battalion Devonshire Regiment. Son of William and Jane Bickle. Died 13th June 1916 and is buried in the Plymouth (Efford) Cemetery. Born in Clovelly and enlisted at Callington (BB)
C21	George Boughton	Born Clovelly. He is on both Bishops Tawton and Teighmouth War Memorials. NEED TO CONFIRM CWGC CERT
C22	Percy William Pengilly	Sick berth Steward 351081 Died 5th June 1916 possiably born at Clovelly. Royal Navy H.MS. 'Hampshire'. A nephew of Tomas Pengilly coxswain of Clovelly life boat. Remembered on Portsmouth Naval Memorial.
C23	C.E. Williams	Second Lieutenant Army Service Corps Died on 17th Oct 1917. He is buried in the Dar Es Salaam War Cemetery Tanzania where 1738 men are remembered. His wife was the daughter of Mrs Marshall of Clovelly High Street
C24	Albert Drury	Company Serjeant Major F/339 of 17th battalion Middlesex regiment. Died 15th Nov 1916. He is remembered on the Varennes Military Cemetery, Somme, France where 1218 men are remembered. North Devon Journal courtesy of BB '28.09.16 Private Ernest Found Royal North Devon Hussers of Clovelly has received a leg wound and is in hospital in Glasgow' '28.09.16 Sergeant Albert Drury (Middlsex Regiment) who has been awarded the Military Cross for 'the conspicuous bravery during the period July 27th-29th is the son in law of Mr Henry Jones of Clovelly' '14.01.17 ... A. Drury company Sergeant Major killed in action ... '

C25	John Manners	Lt. John Neville Manners of the Grenadier Guards 2nd Bn. Died 1st September 1914 age 22. He was the son of John Thomas Manners, 3rd Baron Manners of Avon Tyrell, Christchurch, Hants. and Constance Edwina Adeline Hamlyn-Fane born 28th September 1861 in Clovelly. They married on 12th August 1885 in Clovelly. John was born in London, in 1911 he was living with parents at Avon Tyrell, however in 1901 he was staying with his uncle William Stuckley at Hartland Abbey. J Manners name is inscribed onto the granite war memorial cross at Mount Pleasant at the top of Clovelly high street. 'Mount Pleasant was given to the National Trust by Christine Hamlyn for the use of the people of Clovelly for all time. In memory of those connected with the place who died in the Great War 1914-1918'

CWGC Certificates were not found for Stanley Headon, W Howard and James Somerville, although one was found for 'James Sommerville' but there is little indication that it is the right one so that information has not been used.

www.wwipropaganda.com

YOU SAID
YOU WOULD GO
WHEN YOU WERE
NEEDED

YOU ARE NEEDED
NOW !

Lightning Source UK Ltd.
Milton Keynes UK
UKHW031506090223
416681UK00013B/2965

9 781909 488472